SEE, ANOTH

© G C Davies 1997

First published 1997 by
Nash Pollock Publishing
32 Warwick Street
Oxford OX4 1SX

10 9 8 7 6 5 4 3 2

Orders to:
9 Carlton Close
Grove
Wantage
Oxfordshire OX12 0PU

A catalogue record of this book is available from the British Library

ISBN 1 898255 17 2

Typeset in 11 on 13pt Galliard by Black Dog Design, Buckingham
Cover illustration by Clare Mattey
Printed in Great Britain by TJ International Ltd, Padstow, Cornwall

SEE, ANOTHER DAY

An assembly book for 7-12 year olds

Geoff Davies

Nash Pollock Publishing

Acknowledgments

To my wife, Mollie for reading the stories and narratives and for her patience; my daughter, Susan, Hardwick School, Banbury; my son-in-law, Richard, North Oxfordshire College of Education; Ann Allen, Head of Music at Parsons Down School, Thatcham, for her help and her kind permission to reproduce the music for 'A School Creed' on page 210; Rob Bradford, St Mary's School, Thatcham. And, most of all, to those many children who suffered my own assemblies between 1966 and 1986 – what would I have done without you?

Copyright acknowledgments

Contents

*a 'hedgehog' topic (See 'About this book')

With Year 4 in mind

SCHOOL MATTERS

HOME AND AWAY

THAT'S LIFE!

With Year 5 in mind

SCHOOL MATTERS

HOME AND AWAY

THAT'S LIFE!

With Year 6 in mind

SCHOOL MATTERS

HOME AND AWAY

THAT'S LIFE!

Part 2 Special days: Festivals and Celebrations traditional to the United Kingdom

Part 3 Special days: Festivals and Celebrations originating in cultures not native to the United Kingdom

Appendices

About this book

An assembly, according to most dictionaries, is 'a gathering together, usually with a purpose'. School assemblies have to vary widely to take account of the personality and population of the school and its contributory neighbourhood.

Consequently, the purpose of the assembly will differ from school to school. The purpose may be an act of worship as laid down by law or merely administrative convenience. Where, however, the assembly is for neither of these reasons, it usually features some human frailty, achievement or activity. It is this type of assembly that this book is intended to assist: a resource book that offers a range of themes to which teachers can refer when framing assemblies for children in Years 3 to 6 inclusive. Some of the ideas may be useful when meeting with children in Years 7 and 8.

Teachers using the assemblies are unlikely to regard the material as prescriptive but will select and adapt from the material as they always do.

Because of the significant developmental and social differences between just-seven year olds and near-twelve year olds the assemblies have been arranged so as to appeal more to one chronological age-group than another, but groupings should not be regarded as inviolate. Whoever is conducting the assemblies will, naturally, be the best judges of what suits who and when.

Part 1 (Let us see another day) comprises 72 topics, of story, poem or narrative content, none of which should take longer than four minutes to read or tell, the latter being the preferable form of delivery – if you have the time to prepare it.

Part 2 is made up of assemblies appropriate to use at the times of festivals or celebrations native to the United Kingdom.

Part 3 contains assemblies appropriate to use at the time of festivals or celebrations that have their origins outside the United Kingdom. None of these assemblies attempts theological teaching although a fundamental principle of a faith may be the theme of a story.

Poetry, providing extra reading for use at times of Celebrations are to be found in Appendix 1 on page 211.

Mood music ('coming-in' and 'going-out') is suggested in Appendix 2 on page 223. It is recognised that the musical resources of schools will have to be supplemented from personal collections and that the use of 'mood' music will require some preparation.

Suggestions for songs are drawn mainly from known song books and most songs are repeated from time to time. Again, teachers may well prefer to make their own selections. The titles and sources are collected in Appendix 3 on page 232 for convenience.

A 'Thought to share' is to be found in each assembly. These are included for teachers who are not at ease with 'prayers' for any reason. The prayers ('Are you listening, God?) are monotheistic in address. Other prayers, including prayers for the close of school, are to be found in Appendix 4 on page 236. Two versions of the Lord's Prayer are to be found on pages 238-9.

Starters are suggestions for launching the assembly and are intended to be paraphrased to suit your own situation. It might be as well to look at them before you begin the assembly as you may prefer your own remarks or motivators.

'Hedgehog' topics are 'prickly' topics and are marked with a symbol *. They have been so designated because their content may require the exercise of some discretion on the part of the teacher conducting the assembly – usually because there may be some personal significance to children in the audience.

However you use the book – whether you use the assemblies as they stand or whether you use the parts that are relevant to your aims, bear in mind that all assemblies are more effective if they are uncluttered. The daily corporate act, whether you think of it as worship or not, is not always the best vehicle for 'domestic' announcements. The results of the last netball match or the date of the next jumble sale are better left for other occasions, unless, perhaps, you are making a point about achievement or acting for the good of the school. Even more relevant, you may think the class or departmental assembly is the most sensible occasion on which to make such announcements. It's your school.

PART I

Let us see another day

1
Is it far from Two to Three?

Theme

Welcome to Year 3. Children often need reassurance upon transfer from Infant school or department. They soon recognise that they are now Year 3 and not Year 2, but there is sometimes a period of uncertainty.

Starters

1 Introduce teaching and contact ancillary staff to the children, if this has not already been done.
2 Introduce new staff to all children (or whatever is your school policy).

School geography and school customs are best left for the classroom or group situation.

Story

First day at Markham Hall

The teenagers met at the end of the long drive that led to the Big House.

Thomas grinned and asked, 'Scared?'

Emily replied, 'Of course. My sister says everyone here has to work ever so hard. She's been here for two years.' She was to become a kitchen maid and Thomas was to be a boot boy – the person who cleaned the shoes of the 44 people who lived or worked at the house.

They did not feel too confident when a loud, angry voice, belonging to Gubbins the gardener, bellowed at them from the shrubbery, 'Clear off, you ragamuffins, we don't want the likes of you 'angin' about 'ere.' They ran for their lives, round the back of the Hall where they hid shivering, in a handy doorway.

No sooner had they got their breath back when a gruff voice growled behind them, 'And what might you young scallywags be up to, may I ask?' Emily and Thomas froze with fright but, as the growl became a chuckle, they turned round to see a cheerful woman, wearing a crisp white apron and cap. She stood, arms folded, beaming at the new recruits.

'Bless my soul, a pair of scared rabbits. Come and have some breakfast. You must be Tom and Emily? I'm Mrs Parry, the cook.' Within a few days, they had met all the staff and learnt how to speak to His Lordship and the family and, most important of all, how to do their jobs.

As they walked home together on their first day off, Emily said, 'It seems like we have two homes, now – the Hall and the homes where we have grown up. Mind you, we never had to work so hard before we grew up.'

The message is ...

New places and new people can seem strange and even frightening, but it does not take long to get used to them.

Songs

One more step	*Come & Praise* 47
Morning has broken	*Someone's Singing, Lord* 3 & other books
Use your eyes	*Every Colour* 11

A thought to share

Moving from Year 2 to Year 3 is all part of growing up.

Are you listening, God?

Father God, thank you for the holidays that have now ended. Be with us through the term ahead.

Lord, thank you for our school. Teach us all to be helpful to one another.

Father, help us to work hard and to play well and fairly in this new school year.

2
You're in the
Big Pond now

(*Intended for the new Year 3 only*)

Theme

Adjusting to a new environment with a different pecking order. Some children transferring from Year 2 to Year 3 do not always realise that they are now the little fish in the big pond. The older children will soon remind them of this fact but it is as well if they are prepared for it.

Starters

1 Who knows other children in this school/department?
2 (Selective) Who do you know?
3 What do you think of children in Year 6?
4 When you were Year 2 children did you think you were better than Year 1 children? If so, why?

Story

Number One moves on

Tadpole 89, who is very small, swam cautiously towards Tadpole Number One. The huge tadpole growled, 'What do you want? I'm busy!'

89 squeaked nervously, 'Please, Your Hugeness, can you tell me and my 88 brothers and sisters where your tail has gone?'

Number One snorted impatiently, 'My tail has gone, midget, because I am about to be promoted to be a full frog in the Big Pond. Now push off, it's dinner-time.' A few days later, Number One found that he had a full set of legs. Two hours after that, the ex-Number One, now a very small frog, was sitting on the grassy bank of the Big Pond, waiting to be noticed. As he sat, wondering what to do next, another bigger frog came along.

'Oi, you,' croaked ex-Number One in his new frog-voice, 'Catch me a fly for my breakfast, will you? And be quick about it.' The other frog, whose name is unimportant, croaked with a sinister smile, 'Oh, yes. Blue or green, Fred?'

Ex-Number One snapped, 'My name is not Fred. How dare you speak to me like that? Don't you know who I am?' Then he realised that a crowd of frogs of all sizes and colours was sitting on the opposite bank of the pond, laughing froggily. When the laughter died down, the biggest frog that ex-Number One had ever seen hopped along towards him.

'Not here you aren't, little old boy,' boomed the Queen Frog, for that is what she was, 'You may have been Number One in your small pond. But not in this pond. Here, you are a very small frog indeed. And don't you forget it.'

As it happened, ex-Number One had very little time to forget anything. Later that afternoon he was eaten by a heron. Worst of all, nobody missed him.

The message is ...

'Top dogs' (or are they 'frogs'?) in the Infant school/department world of Year 2 can expect to be at the bottom of the pile when they move to a school or department where there are older and bigger children. New 'Juniors' must recognise that their social relationships are now different.

Songs

This way, that-a-way	*Come & Praise* 53
It's a great, great shame	*Every Colour* 44
Song of the frogs	*Flying a Round* 21
The world is big	*Tinderbox* 33

A thought to share

Are you really the most important person in the world?

Are you listening, God?

Father, help us to remember that, as we grow older, we still have a lot to learn.

Father God, show us how to make new friends and how to learn only good things from them.

Lord, teach us to be good members of our school family.

3
This is our school

Theme

Presenting a 'School Creed' for use in assemblies and on other school occasions.

Reciting the 'School Creed' is a communal act that is not to be construed as a religious act of worship but is an act of 'togetherness', the school being the unifying factor. This 'Creed' may have been used previously in a feeder Infant school or department, but there is no need to omit the 'Starters', unless, of course, you wish to.

Starters

1 Who designs houses?
2 Who builds them?
3 When does a new house become a home?

Story

Many hands make a house

Long ago, in the 13th century, King Edward I of England invaded the land of Wales, which, in those days, was a separate country with its own prince.

The Welsh people, however, said that they would never be ruled by an English king and they fought against the English armies. Edward was angry and sent soldiers into the hills to seek the Welsh fighters. When they could not find the men they took revenge by burning the humble huts of the villagers.

One day the soldiers rode into a tiny village and burnt down every hut, each one made of wattle-and-daub. This is no more than woven willow branches covered in mud, and they are easy to rebuild.

But one poor old widow named Blodwen had not the strength to rebuild her little house and she sat, weeping. Then she was seen by Elen, wife of Tomos, who was once the village blacksmith.

'Why, Blodwen, whatever is the matter?' Elen cried.

'Oh dear,' wailed the old woman, 'I am so old and cold I cannot weave the wattle and I shall have to sleep in the rain tonight. What shall I do?'

'How silly you are,' said Elen, laughing. 'Do you think your friends would leave you with no shelter?' In no time at all, all the women and children and the few old men who were left set to and gathered the withies and covered them with good, thick clay. They made a stout roof of reeds from the edge of the lake in the valley and there was Blodwen's new house, all ready for her to move in.

Not only that, but the women between them made a delicious stew of hare and pigeon for Blodwen and, when it was bubbling and smelling like heaven, they called her in and all had a great feast of stew and new bread, for the villagers had hidden all their grain from the soldiers. Afterwards, Blodwen sang them an old song which in English says, 'You are all my kind friends and your kind hearts have warmed my home for me. Truly, no house is a home unless warm hearts make it so.'

The message is ...

Many hands may build a house but it takes warm hearts to make it a home.

Songs

The building song	*Alleluya* 59
Monday morning	*Songs for Every Day* 6
Place to be	*Tinderbox* 34

A thought to share

This school is an empty, lifeless place when you have all gone home.

A School Creed

This is our school
Let peace live here.
Let the rooms be full of happiness,
Let love be all around,
Love of one another,
Love of all people,
And love of life and living.
Let us remember

That, as many hands build a house,
so many hearts build a school.

This Creed is based on a version used in a one-room Canadian school. You will find music to fit on page 210.

4
What did she say?

Theme

Paying attention when someone is saying something that matters. As we know, children have a very short span of attention …

Starters

1 Greet the children with 'Good Saturday, ladies and gentlemen, I have just landed from the planet Zark. Take me to your leader.'
2 Ask the obvious 'wanderers' what you have just said.
3 Ask someone who was paying attention to repeat this nonsense.
4 Ask why boy X or girl Y could not repeat your speech correctly.

Story

Loud and clear

Phyllis is a little girl with a sunny smile and beautiful manners. One day, she was walking along the path by the river when she saw Claud, her next door neighbour, who was fishing.

He waved and called out to her, 'Can you help, Phyllis, please? Would you go to the fishing shop for me and bring me back a pint of maggots? I can't leave all my fishing gear here. Someone might take it.'

But Phyllis was not really paying attention, not even when he gave her the money. Half an hour later Phyllis returned, and gave Claud a package wrapped in white paper that was hot and smelling of food. The little girl rushed off without even waiting for Claud to say anything.

'Strange maggots,' thought Claud. He unwrapped the package. Inside, to his astonishment was a plastic tray of … faggots-and-peas. Now, in case you don't know what faggots-and-peas are, they are a kind of meat ball with mushy peas and are often sold in fish-and-chip shops and other fast food places.

Claud stood up to call her back, tripped over his fishing-rod and fell into the river with a huge splash and a loud yell. Not only did he fall in but he dragged everything into the water with him – his basket, his stool and his umbrella. As he was holding the faggots-and-peas, they went in with him.

Luckily for him, PC Bottle was passing on his bike, and he fished Claud out of the water just as he was going down for the third time.

Later, when Phyllis was told what had happened she was not at all bothered. 'It was his own stupid fault,' she announced, 'he should have spoken more clearly. I thought he said, "Get some faggots-and-peas" and not "Get some maggots, please." Besides, it was lunchtime. So how was I to know? Especially as I didn't know you used maggots to catch fish. Yuk. Stupid man.'

Of course, Claud could easily have been drowned – all because Phyllis did not bother to listen properly. Not that she saw it like that.

The message is …

It is important to pay attention when you are being spoken to – it might be important.

Songs

When I needed a neighbour	*Come & Praise* 65
On life's highway	*Every Colour* 28
Try again	*Tinderbox* 52

A thought to share

It is far better to listen with one ear than to hear with both ears.

Are you listening, God?

Father, teach us to listen carefully to what people are saying to us.

Lord, we thank you for the gift of hearing. Help us to use it properly.

Father God, show us how to speak carefully so that we shall not be misunderstood.

5
The most important voice

Theme

Monopolising the learning situation.

There is invariably one child who dominates the classroom scene, especially in question and answer sessions. You must know the clarion call of 'Miss, Miss' or whatever rings out above all others. Younger children probably tend to do this more than older ones.

Starters

1   Should children always attempt to answer questions in class?
2   How does one attract attention in order to answer?
3   Why do some children manage to get teacher's attention more than others?

Story

The Moon is a hole in the sky

'And what do you know about it?' said She of the Long White Teeth, which is her Pawnee name, although she is usually called Longteeth. She waved a hand at Little Storm Cloud who was trying to say something.

'Excuse me, Longteeth, I think ...' he squeaked.

Longteeth ignored him and went on, loudly, drowning out his voice, 'Of course the Moon is a hole in the sky. How else could the light from the blue dome above come through? You are not old enough to talk about such mysteries, Cloudy. So shut up and listen to someone who knows what they are talking about.'

Little Storm Cloud waved his arms about and puffed, 'But I'm trying to tell you ...' Longteeth threw a fir cone at him and shook her fist as the boy ran off towards the village.

'You ought to listen,' chattered Crackling Fire, bouncing up and down in excitement.

'Oh, for goodness' sake, Cracky, I'm trying to explain something,' snapped Longteeth. But Cracky had disappeared.

'But, but, but ...' spluttered Swift Arrow, dodging the stone Longteeth threw at him.

'Now, as I was saying,' went on Longteeth, 'Bright Star, will you please stop pulling my skirt?' Her small cousin stopped sucking her thumb and opened and shut her mouth.

'I wasn't doing any such thing!' she protested as she took to her heels. Longteeth sighed, then tried again, 'What is so important that you all have to keep interrupting me? Won't it keep?'

Tall Tree shouted over his shoulder as he bolted into the nearest tepee, 'No, it won't! There's a great big grizzly bear right behind you and it's about to ...'

The message is ...

Why not give someone else a chance to answer a question? There may be times when you are not always right.

Songs

I may speak	*Come & Praise* 100
All the world's a roundabout	*Every Colour* 27
Both sides now	*Alleluya* 33

A thought to share

Not everybody likes your voice as much as you do.

Are you listening, God?

Dear God, help me to understand that not everybody thinks as I do.

Father, teach us to listen to other people's points of view, even if they are different from our own.

Help us, Father God, to understand that our opinion is not the only one

6
I know, I know ...

Theme

Taking advice. All teachers have come across those individuals who know everything, from football tactics to using software or the words of the latest pop song.

Starters

1 Who thinks they can do everything better than other people? Can you justify the claim?

2 Who thinks they can do some things better than other people? Can you justify the claim?

3 Which is the better time to ask for advice? Before you start a project? During? When things go wrong? After you have finished? Or never? Justify the choice.

Story

Nothing to it!

Basil (not his real name, of course) was annoyed because his Mum would not let him help to mix the cake. She had not forgotten cleaning the kitchen ceiling the last time he helped. He wandered to the shed at the end of the garden and opened the door. Just inside was a pile of lovely smooth wood.

'Wow,' breathed Basil, 'Just what I need to build the sledge that Dad has been promising for weeks. This must be the wood for it. I know, I'll save Dad the trouble – I'll make it myself. Nothing to it – bit of glue, a few nails, tin of paint – easy peasy.'

Basil had not stopped to think that the wood was intended for another purpose. Which it was – a garden seat. The wood was teak and very expensive. Basil clambered up on an old stool to get the big box of nails. The wonky leg of the stool gave way just as he was reaching out for them. Basil went one way across the shed and the box of nails went the other, with a deafening crash.

Basil picked the splinters out of his knees, grabbed a handful of nails and began. In the next hour, he cut his thumb (twice) with a chisel which he was not supposed to touch, bruised his foot by dropping the hammer on it, and spilt most of the wood glue on the floor. The rest of the glue found its way into Basil's hair, over his trainers and down his shirt. A little remained to stick the bits of wood together. At last, the sledge was complete. Basil thought it was great. Now for the paint. All he could find was a tin of green.

'That'll do,' muttered Basil, levering off the lid with a screwdriver. He was standing behind the shed door just as he had loosened the lid. What a shame that his father arrived home early from work and decided to go into his shed to get on with his woodwork. The shed door always did stick a bit, so Dad had to give it a hearty shove. Need I finish the story?

The message is ...

Don't be afraid to ask your teacher or other responsible adult for help when you are doing your work.

Songs

If I had a hammer	*Come & Praise* 71
On a work day I work	*Every Colour* 40
Hands to work	*Someone's Singing, Lord* 21

A thought to share

The most foolish people are those who think that they know everything.

Are you listening, God?

Lord, help us to understand that it is right to ask others for good advice.

Father, teach us it is not weakness to ask for help when we need it.

Father God, show us how to share our skills with others.

7
Who needs rules?

Theme

Are school rules (codes of conduct, codes of behaviour or whatever your school may call them) necessary? Most schools have a 'guidance' framework to which children are expected to conform. Such guidance may be written or unwritten but, however the school regards this aspect of policy, children should realise that they have obligations to the school community.

Starters

Teacher: Your treatment of the introduction to this assembly will depend on your current school policy. The following 'Starters' relate to schools that already have some 'conduct norms' in place.

1 Should schools have rules? (or codes of conduct/behaviour)
2 What should they be?
3 If there are no school rules how are children to know what are and are not acceptable standards of behaviour?
4 Suggest what could replace rules.
5 Who should frame school rules? Why?

Story

Nobody needs to tell *me*

Rosie was in a foul temper as she stormed into the cloakroom. 'That stupid old Mr Hunt has taken my new gold necklace off me,' she said, almost in tears. 'He said that it's against school rules to bring expensive jewellery to school. As if I'm not grown up enough to look after it! Stupid rules!'

'I reckon we should go and see Mrs Richards and say that we all think school rules should be abolished,' announced Janine. 'I got told off yesterday for having dangly earrings. What's the harm in them, anyway?'

It was two days before they drummed up the courage to visit the headteacher. Not too many friends were keen to join them. Robbie Parry said he liked the head he had got and Sanjay Patel said he didn't want to be eaten alive. So the two girls went on their own.

To their astonishment, Mrs Richards smiled and listened carefully to their complaints. Even more amazing, she said she would see what she could do about it. Next day, in assembly, she said she was scrapping school rules. The whole school could hardly believe it. But it was true.

The day after that, ten minutes after assembly, Matthew Davies crashed into Sandra Grant as he ran out of the library. At lunchtime, Darren Harper cut his knee on a broken bottle of cola, Tom Williams had trodden on David Rummins' new remote-control car and then there had been a fight. Ah Chim had broken Jo Rankin's new CD walkman and … the list was endless.

By going-home time, there was a crowd of children knocking on Mrs Richards' door asking please could they have their school rules back because everybody was fed up with breakages and fights and accidents and they could all see why there were school rules in the first place.

Mrs Richards agreed, with another, different smile. But you don't believe this story, do you? Well, the school is in … no, I'd better not say …

The message is …

Schools could be chaotic places if there was no guidance about behaviour at all.

Songs

A living song	*Come & Praise* 72
Working together	*Every Colour* 37
Both sides now	*Alleluya* 32

A thought to share

If everybody respected everyone else, would we need any rules?

Are you listening, God?

Father God, teach us to respect other people and their property.

Lord, show us how to live without hurting others.

Dear God, make us good members of the school family and caring members of our community.

8
It may be a game to you*

Theme

Teasing. Children of all ages and backgrounds indulge in teasing, not always aware of how hurtful it can be to the victim. It is, in fact, a form of bullying and children should be made aware of how cruel it can be.

Starters

1 Has anyone ever been teased, other than innocently?
2 What were you teased about?
3 Was the teasing hurtful?
4 Who has ever teased anyone? Why?
5 Why do you think people tease one another (it is not only children)?

Story

Teacher: You may need to consider your own school population before reading this story.

The whispering boy

Marco was a quiet boy who kept himself to himself. He was never rude to other children nor to his teachers. He did not pick fights nor criticise people who lived in houses. I say this, because Marco lived in a brightly-painted caravan, pulled along by a patient old mare. This is how gypsies lived in the years we call the Thirties, before the Second World War.

His family had camped near the village and his parents had sent him to the school so that he could learn to read and write – which he was doing very quickly indeed. But, oh! How the village children made it so clear just what they thought of traveller children. Marco was teased by a gang of children, led by the two biggest boys in the school, day after day.

'Didicoi, didicoi, who's a dirty gypsy boy?' was one of their chants as a big group of children danced round the boy in a sneering ring. Marco never rose to the bait, but, as soon as he was able, walked away and sat in a corner of the playground.

But all was to change on one Friday morning. As the usual gang of children performed their vicious taunts, there was a terrific commotion as children screamed and yelled and ran in all directions. The two teasing ringleaders ran faster than anyone else, not caring about anyone else. Everyone was running away from a huge, black horse that had leapt over the school fence and was galloping crazily around the playground. Several children fell in their panic and seemed to be in danger of being trampled under the animal's hoofs.

Except Marco. Quick as a flash, he grabbed the reins that dangled from the horse's neck and, somehow, swung himself into the saddle. The gypsy boy leaned forward and whispered into the horse's ear, as it raced around the yard. The animal's crazy charge slowed to a shivering, sweating halt.

Marco slipped off its back and blew gently up the horse's nostrils, in between whispering words in a strange language. The frightened children looked on as the big horse nuzzled Marco with its soft nose.

Do you think anyone teased Marco after that?

The message is ...

People who practise teasing are bullies.

Songs

It's a new day	*Come & Praise* 106
Take care of a friend	*Every Colour* 35
Don't you push me down	*Tinderbox* 26

A thought to share

Put yourself in the place of the person you have been teasing. Isn't it fun?

Are you listening, God?

Lord, teach us to be kind to others, even if we don't like them.

Father, give us the strength to stand up for those who cannot stand up for themselves.

Father God, help us to do all the good we can
By all the means we can in all the ways we can
At all the times we can to all the people we can
As long as ever we can.

(after John Wesley)

HOME AND AWAY

9
Square Eyes

Theme

Watching too much television. This lighthearted poem offers a 'doom' scenario but it is a fact that too many children watch too much TV unselectively.

Starters

1 How many children watch TV for more than one hour a day? How much? Why?
2 How many children never watch TV? Why?
3 Who thinks that watching a lot of TV is not a good idea?
4 What else can you do instead of watching TV?

Poem

Whatever happened to Spiro Speen?
An eight year old named Spiro Speen
Just lived to watch the tele screen;
Commercials, quizzes, teletext,
His only question, 'What's on next?'
He ate his meals and viewed non-stop,
Music programmes, rock and pop;
BBC and Channel Four,

Cable, satellite and much more.
Spiro watched the news and soaps
Until his parents gave up hope
Of Spiro being of any use.
His granny cried, 'You silly goose!'
But Spiro said, 'Don't be a bore,
Ah, football's on, now what's the score?'
The welfare lady came to call,
For Spiro never went to school at all.
His parents had to go to court
But Spiro gave them not a thought.
The magistrate said, 'Pay a fine,
A hundred pounds it is this time,
Next time you both shall go to jail.'
The parents went extremely pale,
But all their son was heard to cry
Was 'Snooker's on at five on Sky!'
Poor Mr Speen said to his wife,
'Our son is wasting all his life.'
His wife agreed, 'We must be firm.
I know the boy will yell and squirm,
But that TV must go tonight.'
Her husband said, 'Yes, yes, quite right.'
They called the shop that very day
To take the TV set away.
They came and disconnected it.
Young Spiro had a screaming fit;
He howled and then attacked the man
And hit him with a frying pan.
The man fell down and hit his head
And, as he bled, he sternly said,
'You've really done it now, young Speen,'
And soon police were on the scene.

They put the boy into a van
Still screeching at the TV man.
He's not been seen since, anywhere,
No, not a sausage, hide nor hair.
For two whole days his parents grieved,
But they were secretly relieved.
Their son has disappeared from view,
So beware TV – it could be you!

The message is ....

It's staring you in the face ...

Songs

Time is a thing	*Come & Praise* 104
There's so much pleasure	*Every Colour* 10
All night, all day	*Alleluya* 75

A thought to share

How ever did children amuse themselves before television was invented?

Are you listening, God?

Father, we thank you for the wonders of technology. Help us to make the best use of inventions like television and computers.

Father God, help us to develop interests in many things.

Thank you, Lord, for the talents of inventors who have made so many things possible.

10
Or would you rather be ... *

Theme

The delicate subject of cleanliness. Some children do not always seem to be aware of the need for personal responsibility when it comes to cleanliness.

Starters

Teacher: It goes without saying that you may need to exercise some tact here, especially if there is a school problem.

1   What brand of soap is used at home?
2   Who uses something other than soap?
3   Who prefers to shower instead of bathing? (Any general questions about washing etc. will do.) You may prefer to leave these next starters for the classroom:
4   Did people always bath/shower regularly as most people do, nowadays?
5   Do you think people in olden days might have been rather smelly?
6   If they were, how did they disguise it?

Story

The pink stranger

Warthogs are not the prettiest of animals but they do like being sweet and clean. The herd that lived near the lazy River Polumpopo in Tanzania was no exception. Every morning, as the sun was waking up, the herd charged down to the river, scattering the pink flamingoes and the long-legged weaver birds. If there were no hungry crocodiles about, looking for breakfast, into the water they thundered, there to wallow and splash and frolic, making a joyful noise and a lot of mess.

Then, one morning after the Great Rains were over, a strange little pink creature appeared in the midst of the herd, fast asleep with the warthoglets. None of the herd knew where it had come from, nor when it had arrived. The little stranger seemed to be so frightened and Big Boar, chief of the herd, had not the heart to send it away.

So he let it stay and gave it the name of 'The Pink One' as it seemed to know no name of its own. The little fellow soon became like the rest of the warthogs, grunting, snorting and eating the same food.

Yet, in one respect, it was different from all the rest. The Pink One would not join in the morning bathe, making all sorts of excuses. Before long, the warthogs began to avoid The Pink One, making remarks about an unpleasant smell that seemed to follow the stranger wherever it went.

The poor little animal went to Big Boar and asked him why his new friends avoided him. The chief warthog explained that all warthogs bathed every day. Otherwise, they would smell … just like some other animal of which he had heard but never seen. The Pink One had no idea what kind of creature he meant and, so far as I know, he still does not. He joins in the morning splash and the unpleasant smell has vanished. I cannot say what kind of creature the Big Boar meant, for even I am not certain.

Perhaps you are able to tell me?

The message is …

Most children of today are aware of personal hygiene but, now and again, there is a maverick.

Songs

Water of life	*Come & Praise* 2
Because you care	*Every Colour* 31
Think, think on these things	*Someone's Singing, Lord* 38

A thought to share

It has been said that coal miners used to believe that too much bathing weakened their backs. Is it true?

Are you listening, God?

Father of us all, help us to be clean in mind and body.

Thank you, Lord, for our wonderful bodies. Show us how to care for them in the best way that we can.

Father God, help us to remember that our bodies will not look after themselves but that we must treat them with respect.

11
Up the wooden hill!

Theme

Keeping late hours. Too many children do not go to bed as early as they should. Television viewing is probably the main reason and teachers can usually identify those children who do not get enough sleep.

Starters

1 Who goes to bed before 8pm? Why?
2 Who goes to bed after 8 pm? Why?
3 Who goes to bed much later than that – not occasionally but regularly?
4 Is the old saying true: 'Early to bed and early to rise, makes a man (person) healthy, wealthy and wise?'
5 What else is there to gain from going to bed at an early hour?

Story

Clarissa takes a little nap

Clarissa did not like going to bed. Winter or summer, if the clock had not struck ten, she made a fuss about it. The nine-year old described any bedtime before ten o'clock as ridiculous, crazy, silly, childish, unreasonable, nonsense and boring, especially boring. Yet, for some strange reason, Clarissa was always tired.

One fine July day, her class set off to visit Ramwell Zoo. Clarissa fell asleep on the coach, she fell asleep in the café where they had been allowed to leave their packed lunches and she fell asleep on the bench while her teacher was sorting the children into groups. Her friend woke her up just as her group were moving off. The group trotted after Mrs Webb, a volunteer Mum, with Clarissa dawdling behind, yawning and rubbing her eyes. She was so busy being tired that she walked through an open gate, saw a tree stump, sat down behind it and … yes, you've guessed it, went to sleep in an animal's cage.

The silly girl did not realise that the gate had been left open by an equally silly keeper. He had broken all the rules of the Zoo but, as he said later, he had only nipped out for a second. How was he to know that a school party was around?

Now, just imagine how you would feel, if you were woken up from a little nap by a very large … very furry hand, stroking your hair. Clarissa's piercing scream frightened the gorilla so much that she shot into her den and refused to come out for three days. Clarissa, meanwhile, had never moved so fast and she was back on the coach, hiding under the seat before you could say forty winks.

I shall leave it to your imagination as to whether she stayed up late at night again. I will tell you, though, that the keeper lost his job, which may seem a little unfair.

As for Gloria, the gorilla, she was never quite the same again ….

The message is ..

Many children will scoff at this story – they always know what's best for them. You could always suggest that they keep their wits about them the next time they visit a zoo.

Songs

All night, all day	*Alleluya* 75
Look around	*Every Colour* 9
Hay ho! Time to go to bed	*Flying a Round* 14

A thought to share

Aren't you glad *you* have a bed to sleep in?

Are you listening, God?

Thank you, God, for the blessing of sleep that refreshes us for the demands of each new day.

We thank you, Lord, for our beds and a roof over our heads.
Let us remember that many people have neither.

Father, God, thank you for being with us through the night and when we wake.

12
Only a fib

Theme

Emphasising that a lie is a lie whatever euphemism is used instead. No matter whether a lie is called a porkie (rhyming slang – pork pie = lie), a fib, a whopper, a tall story or even – if you really want to stun your listeners – a terminological inexactitude, it is still ... a lie.

Starters

1 What words are often used for the word 'lie'?
2 Is a lie any the less because a euphemism is used?

Story

Everard's tell-tale ears

Mr Simkin was a jeweller who sold and mended clocks and watches. He also sold jewellery. His assistant, Everard, was learning to be a watch-mender and jeweller and he was doing well, but he had a terrible memory.

One morning, Mr Simkin opened up his shop and found that everything had been stolen during the night. The burglars had even taken the kettle used for making the tea – and the tea itself. Of course, the police came and asked questions.

'You are quite certain, Everard,' said Detective Trudge, 'That you checked the windows and locked the doors?' Everard was quite positive that he had.

'And you switched on the burglar alarm?' asked the detective.

Everard looked most uncomfortable and gulped, 'Of course I did. As if I would forget that.'

'Funny,' muttered Trudge, 'I wonder why the alarm didn't go off at the police station?' Everard lost his temper and started to shout that he was telling the truth.

'In that case, Everard,' said Mr Simkin, quietly, 'Why have your ears gone red? They always go red when you are telling lies. Isn't that so?'

Everard, although he was sixteen years old, burst into tears and whined, 'Sorry, Mr Simkin, I'm sorry. But I only told a little fib. I didn't want to be blamed for the burglary.'

Mr Simkin looked very angry. 'You did not tell a fib, young man,' he said, sadly, 'You told … a deliberate lie and no other word will do.' Everard was so ashamed that he ran out of the shop and never went back.

The burglar was caught and sent to prison but the loot was never found – the burglar forgot where he had buried it. Mr Simkin collected the insurance, sold the shop and went to live in Spain. As for Everard, he joined the army and never told a lie again. You don't believe me? Well, next time you visit Buckingham Palace, have a look at the ears of the guardsmen on duty outside and see if any of them have got red ears.

The message is …

Liars usually give themselves away.

Songs

It's a new day	*Come & Praise* 106
Take the time to cogitate	*Every Colour* 47
You and I	*Tinderbox* 56

A thought to share

The trouble with lying is that the liar, in time, comes to believe the lies.

Are you listening, God?

Lord, help us to be truthful at all times.

Dear God, teach us the difference between truth and falsehood.

Father of us all, show us that our family and friends are more likely to trust us if they know they can believe what we tell them.

13
At the table*

Theme

Acceptable table manners. Different cultures have different ways of conveying food to the mouth and eating it. Table manners vary the world over and what is acceptable for one culture is distasteful to another. In the United Kingdom, traditional English manners require the use of knife and fork and restrained mastication. Those of us who have experienced the school meals scene will recognise departures from the norm …

Starters

1 What are 'table manners'?
2 How can an eater offend other people?
3 Are table manners the same the world over?
4 Are table manners the same all over this country?
5 Are table manners the same in different homes?

Story

The explorer's cutlery

Walter said that he had found the few tattered pages of the diary on a market stall in Quito, the capital city of Ecuador in South America. He began to read from them.

'*15 May 1788* The last of my food ran out three days ago and I am an unhappy man. I hear mysterious noises and can feel that I am being watched. They are, I fear … (here the words were blotted out by a dark stain.)

19 May 1788 I have been taken prisoner but these native Indians (I know not what else to call them) have shown me great kindness. They bring me tasty food of all descriptions and I declare that I am becoming quite plump. Today, one of the old men came and pinched my leg, after which he went out of the hut, nodding, rubbing his hands, and smacking his lips. I do not understand these strange customs.

24 May 1788 These primitive folk seem to be fascinated by my use of knife and fork for the eating of my food. These were a gift from my dear mother on the day of my departure. The natives hoot with merriment when I stick my fork into a piece of meat and when I cut off a suitable portion and convey it to my mouth they roll on the floor, helpless with laughter. Not only that, but they consider my manner of eating silently with mouth closed and my use of a linen napkin to be so disgusting that they have to leave my presence.

22 June 1788 My mealtimes become embarrassing as the whole village gathers to watch me eating. Men, women and children bring their own food and eat it in my hut. They pick up all food with their fingers and this they munch with much smacking of lips and open mouths so as to make as much noise as possible. They wipe their mouths with the backs of their hands and suck their fingers most loudly and belch thunderously when they have eaten but a few mouthfuls. I have learnt from one of their number, through sign language, that they regard their conduct as being exceedingly good manners.'

Walter closed the book and said, shaking his head, 'There are no more pages. Nobody knows what happened to this man, whoever he was. But the old woman who sold me the diary told me that, long ago, the people who lived in the jungle were … cannibals.'

The message is …

Acceptable standards for table manners vary from culture to culture but there is no reason why children should not learn what those standards are, at home or at school.

Songs

Rabbit ain't got	*Apusskidu* 37
The hungry man	*Every Colour* 32
A time for everything	*Songs for every Day* 25

A thought to share

How many people actually enjoy watching others eating their food?

Are you listening, God?

Lord, help us to understand that what we think is acceptable behaviour can upset other people.

Dear God, thank you for our food. Give us the wisdom to realise that it is a gift from you and that we should never waste food.

Father God, teach us to be good neighbours, remembering that many of the things that we do or say can affect others.

━━━━━━━━━━ THAT'S LIFE! ━━━━━━━━━━

14
The big hand is on ...

Theme

All Year 4 children should be able to tell the time. A surprising number of children cannot tell the time from an analogue-type watch or clock and the 24-hour clock is a mystery to many. The assembly should be followed up in the classroom.

Starters

1 Who can tell the time on an ordinary clock with hands? (Check if you like)

2 Who can tell me the 24-hour time – now?

3 Does it matter if you can't tell the time? Why?

Story

Jarvis and the watch

Jarvis had never been so excited in his life. What a birthday he was having! The family were off to Disneyland in a few hours' time.

It had been a brilliant day so far. Grandad had given him a new mountain bike for his ninth birthday and there had been all sorts of presents from relatives, including a very impressive-looking watch from Auntie Sue. Strangely, Jarvis was not very excited about that.

Anyway, the mountain bike just had to be shown to his best friend Clyde that very afternoon, before the family left for Florida.

He was about to bolt through the door after lunch when his mother called to him from the kitchen.

'Jarvis! We have to be at Heathrow two hours before the flight. We must leave here no later than three o'clock. Just make sure ...'

But her son had gone, pedalling like mad on his way to his mate's house. He need not have hurried. When he got there, Clyde had gone out. Jarvis rode home, rather annoyed.

Then, as he cycled past Dark Wood, he saw the flash of reddish-brown. High in the big oak tree on the edge of the woods. Then again. More than a flash this time. He could see a bushy tail. No mistake. It was the same colour as a fox. But foxes don't climb trees. It *had* to be a *red squirrel*. Jarvis couldn't believe his eyes.

He muttered excitedly to himself, 'There haven't been red squirrels in these woods for years. Not since Dad was a kid. He told me they might be trying to bring 'em back.' The squirrel made one final appearance in the bright sunlight and then vanished into the green darkness.

Frantically Jarvis charged into the woods, bouncing and bumping as he rode. He rode round and round for ages, staring up at the trees until his neck ached, hoping to catch another glimpse of the rare creature and only falling off twice. Despite his efforts, there was no sign of the squirrel. It was when he hit a tree root and fell off for the third time, with a crash that left him quite dazed, that the intrepid hunter decided he had better give up and go home.

But Jarvis felt quite sick as he picked up his bike. Three horrible thoughts came into his mind. One was that he must have chased the squirrel for miles, deep into the woods. Secondly, the crash had bent his front wheel. And, last but not least, he had no idea what time it was.

Yes, I know he had a watch. A fine watch, with bright red hands and figures. But it was no use his looking at it. *Jarvis had no idea what time it was.* That's right. Nine years old and he could not tell the time. Oh, crikey, he was going to miss the flight. The family wouldn't go without him. Would they?

He began to cry, but soon realised that tears would do no good, so he set off for home, pushing his damaged bike.

They got to the airport just in time to watch the jumbo jet taking off.

Would you be surprised to know that Jarvis was not very popular with the rest of the family? Dad managed to book a week in a caravan in Bognor. That would have been better than nothing. But it rained every day.

And all because ... well, you tell me.

The message is ...

Being unable to tell the time is something that could cause serious problems.

Songs

All night, all day	*Alleluya* 75
My grandfather's clock	*Ta-ra-ra-boom-de-ay* 54
Song of the clock	*Tinderbox* 7

A thought to share

You can't have time back once it's gone.

Are you listening, God?

Lord, show us how to use our time to do the best we can.

Dear God, thank you for clocks and watches and for the skill of the people who make them.

Thank you, God, for all that we learn at school. Help us to put all our knowledge to good use.

15
Have a care!

Theme

Playing in dangerous places. Children often play games in any place that takes their fancy without due regard to any hazards that may be present.

Starters

1 Who has a favourite place to play?
2 Is it safe?
3 Do you know anyone who plays in unsafe places? (No names)

4 Suggest some places where children play, that are unsafe.

5 Suggest some places where it is safe to play.

Story

A cold bath

This is based on a true story, although names and locations have been changed – but there are many true stories just like it.

Charlie and Kenny slid along the icy road, looking for adventure on this wonderful, sunny, sparkling white, snowy, icy morning. They couldn't believe it when they arrived at the Lower Pond near the brickworks. The shining ice could hardly be seen for children and grown-ups, skating, sliding and falling over, so the boys decided to look for somewhere less crowded.

'Let's try the Old Pond at the top of Crown Street', said Charlie. After trudging the half-mile up the hill, they were delighted to find that the frozen pond was deserted.

Kenny said, his eyes shining with excitement, 'Looks great. Do you reckon the ice is OK?'

'Huh,' grunted, Charlie, 'It had better be. Chips Woodward says the water here is a hundred feet deep.' Kenny gave him a shove and rushed on to the ice, with a whoop of glee. Charlie was close behind him and, for an hour, they slid and slipped and tumbled. Then, disaster struck ...

As they had a competition to see who could slide farthest without falling over, Kenny reached the middle of the pond. Ignoring the ominous creaking of the ice, he waved his arms in triumph. There was a sinister cracking noise and he disappeared with a yell as the ice gave way.

Charlie stood there with his mouth open, having no idea what to do. As he gaped in disbelief, his pal's head re-appeared, spluttering and shouting for help. Charlie crept gingerly towards him, then, without warning, the ice collapsed beneath his feet, pitching him into the water, too. Even through his clothes, the water was cold enough to take his breath away and he thrashed about in the water, quite forgetting the predicament of his friend.

It was just as well that they had been seen. Ted Miles had seen them take their icy bath as he tied a ladder on to the roof of his old van. Brave man that he was, he managed to reach the teeth-chattering, frozen lads and to drag them out of the water. He thawed them out in front of a blazing fire in his house and took them home, giving them a lecture on the way. The boys' dads did more than give them a lecture. Not that they needed a good walloping to remind them how stupid they had been on that January day, which could have been their last.

How do I know all this? I'm Charlie and this all happened in 1935 when I was ten years old. You don't forget things like that, do you?

The message is ...

Think before you play in places that might be dangerous. And you know what is likely to be safe and what is not.

Songs

It's a new day	*Come and Praise* 106
We will take care of you	*Every Colour* 36
Taking my time	*Songs for Every Day* 61

A thought to share

When you take risks, stop and think that other people might get hurt, too.

Are you listening, God?

Lord, teach us to listen to advice from those who know better than we do.

Dear God, be with us as we play. Help us to be sensible in our choice of places to play.

Father God, be good to me. The world is so big and I am so small, even if I think I am not.

16
Superman may be bullet-proof

Theme

Relating screen images to reality. Too many children, even at Year 3 and Year 4 level, fail to distinguish between screen 'action', such as Batman, Superman or whatever characters are enjoying contemporary popularity, and real life.

Starters

On the whole, fictional 'heroes', especially fantasy characters, come and go, and you may like to refer to the current trends for the purposes of this theme.

1 If Bugs Bunny (say) fell off a cliff would he really get up and walk away?
2 If Batman (say) as played by an actor, is 'zapped' by a missile, does he really bleed?
3 Would the actor be in pain? Why not?
4 If a soldier is shot or blown up, does he hurt and bleed? Might he die? Why?
5 If you were shot, would you hurt? Would you bleed? Why?

Story

The character of 'Aeroman' does not exist (yet).

The Adventures of Aeroman

The heads of the shoppers jerked upwards as if they were puppets. The scream that had attracted their attention came from the roof of the multi-storey car park, thirty metres above the crowded shopping precinct. No sooner had the shriek died away than a horrified gasp rushed from the crowd.

'Oh, no! Look!' whispered a woman shopper, pointing towards the top floor. She, and the rest of the crowd, stared at a little figure that was dancing on the low wall that edged the roof of the car park.

'It's a kid!' spluttered a busker. 'He can only be four years old.' A woman's voice was heard, faintly, from the roof, pleading with the child, 'Please, darling, get off the wall. Mummy won't be cross with you. Just come down, please and we'll go and buy a new toy.'

The little boy shrilled, 'I'm Aeroman, I'm Aeroman!' An' I can fly just like he does on the video an' I'm going to splat Molewoman wiv my jetblaster! Do you want to see me fly, Mummy, it's ever so easy?' The small figure spread his arms and began to make 'aeroplane' noises, swooping and swaying along the parapet, conscious of no danger as he became Aeroman, in his own little world of fantasy. Then he swooped and swayed once too often. Before he could tumble off his lofty perch a uniformed arm had scooped him, yelling and arms flailing and he disappeared from view. A policeman appeared on the roof and gave a 'thumbs-up' sign, together with a broad grin.

A sigh of relief came from the watching crowd and they went about their business. 'That was close,' said the woman from the greetings-card shop. 'Yeah,' agreed a tattooed young man, scratching his bristly scalp. 'Still, the kid would soon have found out that he couldn't fly, wouldn't he?'

'That's true,' puffed Tony, who runs the pizza parlour, 'But I guess he wasn't old enough to know any better.'

The message is ...

Little children often confuse fantasy with reality. You are too grown up to do this.

Songs

A living song	*Come & Praise* 72
My mind to me a kingdom is	*Every Colour* 18
Mysteries	*Tinderbox* 40

A thought to share

Only those who invent stories create fictional characters. They can kill them off, too.

Are you listening, God?

Lord, teach us what is real and what is not.

Thank you, God, for authors and artists. Help us to remember that fiction is only someone's imagination.

We are grateful, Father God, for the wonders of television, films and videos. Show us how to follow good examples in the things we see and to turn our backs on those that are evil.

17
We can all be good at something

Theme

Don't put yourself down. Everyone possess a gift of some kind, even if it is no more than making someone else happy.

Starters

1 Who can fly an aeroplane? Why not?
2 Who can speak Portuguese? (You may need some research ...)
3 Who knows the names of all the planets?
4 Who can spell 'diplodocus'?
5 Who can swim?
6 Who can say their six times multiplication table?
7 Who knows how to call an ambulance on the telephone?
(*Teacher*: You may have some more relevant questions than these)
8 Who thinks they can't do anything? Are you sure?
9 Who thinks that everyone can do something well?

Story

If you think that you can't do anything, perhaps this story will make you think of something that you can.

The Sons of Owen

('Rhys' is pronounced as if it rhymes with 'grease'.)

Long ago, so I have been told, there lived, in the old Princedom of Wales, a noble lord by the name of Owen. He had three fine sons, Tomos, Tudor and Rhys.

Tomos, the eldest, was an amazing archer, who could split an apple in two at a hundred paces. Tudor, the middle son, was a great swimmer who could swim across the icy lake that sulked near their village. Indeed, he could do this not once, but twice, without stopping for a rest.

As for Rhys, the youngest, he believed he could do none of these things. His archery was wild – if he aimed at an apple he would be fortunate to hit the tree, and he turned blue in cold water.

'Father,' he said one night after supper, 'Why can't I do the things that my brothers find so simple?' His father looked at him with much love, for Rhys was the apple of his Father's eye.

'You will find your own gifts, my son,' he said, with a smile. As he said this, his eye fell upon the great harp that stood in the corner of the room, dusty and neglected.

'Why do you not pluck upon the strings of that old harp?' he asked, raising a bushy eyebrow. 'It has not sounded since Madoc the Bard left to be minstrel to the Great Prince of Wales. For no one here can make the harp sing.' (I must explain that, in the Welsh language, the word 'sing' is the same word as 'play'.) Rhys turned up his freckled nose and wailed that he could never do such a clever thing because he could do nothing, nothing at all.

'You have nothing to lose by trying,' said his father and so Rhys tried his luck. He was so encouraged by his first efforts that Rhys took lessons from Gwyn, Master of the Harp, an old harpist from the village. What is more, Rhys discovered that his voice was as sweet as the harp's singing.

It took many lessons and a great deal of practice before Rhys became a true minstrel. And, before he reached his twentieth birthday, he went on to become Chief Minstrel to the Prince of Wales, in the steps of Madoc who had retired. It came as no surprise to Owen that his son became known as Rhys, the Great Bard and all manner of people marvelled at the his skill that gave joy to so many folk.

The message is …

Everyone can do something well – why not find out what it is?

Songs

Simple gifts	*Come & Praise* 97
I can climb	*Every Colour* 17
Hands to work	*Someone's Singing*, Lord 21

A thought to share

You will never know what you can do until you try.

Are you listening, God?

Thank you, God, for all the talents that we have been given, even if we do not always realise what they are.

Teach us, good Lord, to use the skills we have learned, to help others.

Father God, thank you for our school, where we learn how to put our talents to good use.

18
I just called *

Theme

Overcoming visual impairment. This assembly takes a brief look at the pop star Stevie Wonder.

Starters

1 Could you write a song, sing it and accompany yourself on the piano?
2 Would it be even more difficult to do if you could not see at all?
3 Who knows the name of a well-known American singer who is unable to see but can do all those things? (You can give a few clues – His names begin with 'S' and 'W' and he is black.)

4 Who can name a musician who cannot hear? (Evelyn Glennie; see Assembly 54 (with Year 5 in mind).
5 Suggest some things that visually- or hearing-impaired people might be able to do better than sighted or hearing people

Narrative

Little Stevie Wonder

Not everybody likes the kind of music composed, played and sung by Stevie Wonder. Nobody, however, can fail to appreciate his remarkable achievements in overcoming blindness to become an international star in the world of popular music.

He was born in Michigan, USA in 1950 and his real name is Steveland Judkin Morris. He was never to see his four brothers and one sister, because he had no sight from birth. Even as a little boy, he sang in the Whitestone Baptist chapel choir and, by the age of five, he had begun to learn piano, keyboards, harmonica, drums and bongos. Steveland spent many hours listening to all kinds of music and paid particular attention to the music of a blind singer and pianist called Ray Charles.

The boy went to the Fitzgerald school for the Blind in Detroit. At the age of ten, he was introduced to the man who was the best-known producer of records of the music that is called 'Tamla Motown'. At the age of eleven, he made his first record, called 'I call it pretty music' but it was not a success.

Calling himself 'Little Stevie Wonder', by the time he was thirteen he was successful on stage and had cut his first big record, called 'The 12-year old genius'. This reached Number One in the American pop charts. Later, he dropped the 'Little' from his name and went on to become famous all over the world, his records selling in millions, which made him a very rich man.

Stevie was nearly killed in 1974 in a car smash but he recovered and is still performing to big audiences today. His most famous record, 'I just called to say I love you', is one of the top 10 biggest-selling singles of all time. This remarkable man has organised charity concerts of all kinds, especially for people with disabilities and he has done a great deal of work for visually-impaired children.

The message is …

If Stevie Wonder can become world famous without sight, just think what you can do.

Songs

Look around	*Every Colour* 9
He gave me eyes	*Someone's Singing, Lord* 19
Until I saw the sea	*Tinderbox* 38

A thought to share

Sight is a most precious gift, but some people can do wonders without it.

Are you listening, God?

Thank you, Lord, for being able to see and hear and for our other senses. Show us how to help people who cannot do what we can do.

Dear God, open our eyes to what is beautiful and our minds to what is good.

For eyes to look to you,
For ears to hear your word,
For feet to walk in your ways,
For lips to sing your praise,
For hands to do your will,
For hearts to love you still,
We thank you, God.

With Year 4 in mind

SCHOOL MATTERS

19
An away day

Theme

Absenteeism. Most children who are absent from school have genuine reasons for being away. Although it tends to be less of a problem in primary than secondary schools, it should be made clear that avoidable absence is not acceptable behaviour.

Starters

1 Give some good reasons for being away from school.
2 Why is absence from school sometimes a bad thing?
3 Who loses out when you are away from school?

Story

Teacher: You may care to remind children that life in the 1930s was, for many children, a hard time. This was especially so when parents were unemployed and the State benefits of those days were far from generous. Schools were not very jolly places – teachers were very strict and children were caned for all sorts of reasons. Anyone absent from school had to have a very good reason for it.

This story is based on a true incident, although names and location have been changed.

No boots, Sir

The teacher put down his pen, put the top back on the red ink bottle, closed the register and glared around the classroom. Each one of the forty-eight boys in the class tried to avoid his beady eye.

Mr Wilkins boomed, 'And where might Stanley Hilditch be today, may I ask?" Nobody was keen to answer. But Billy Pearce had the misfortune to sneeze. That was enough for the stern teacher.

'Yes, boy?' he barked, 'So where is Hilditch, then?' He left his high desk and stood over the trembling eleven year old.

'Dunno, Sir,' muttered Billy.

'Don't lie to me, boy,' bellowed Wilkins, poking Billy in the ribs with the sharp end of his blackboard pointer.

'I don't, Sir, honest, Sir, I don't,' Billy yelped even more loudly. Mr Wilkins was about to inflict another painful prod when the stick was snatched from his hand and thrown on to the floor. The stunned teacher swung round in disbelief, his face almost purple with fury. Glaring at him, teeth gritted and fists clenched, was Jimmy Burchell, the biggest boy in the class.

'He don't know. But I do!' he growled. The teacher stood, staring at Jimmy as if hypnotised. The pointer lay on the floor, where he had dropped it.

Jimmy went on, 'Stanley ain't 'ere because 'e ain't got no boots. His Dad was killed down the pit last June month and his Ma ain't got no money to buy new ones and he can't come to school until his old boots has been repaired. Now go on, 'it me, I don't care.'

But Mr Wilkins did no such thing. Instead, he went silently back to his seat and finished marking the register. On Thursday, Stanley reappeared at school, wearing a pair of brand new, shiny-bright black boots. They had appeared on his front doorstep the night before and no one could imagine where they had come from. Would you like to make a guess?

The message is ...

Most children stay away from school for a good reason. But some do not.

Songs

Don't you think we're lucky	*Every Colour* 25
Each day different	*Harlequin* 43
Newspaper pictures	*Songs for Every Day* 25

A thought to share

It is surprising just how many children get bored during the school holidays.

Are you listening, God?

Dear Lord, thank you for our school and for all that we learn here.

Please, God, help us to make the most of all the chances we are given and let us never waste a single moment.

Remind us now and again, Father God, that schools are built for children.

20
Reasons and excuses

Theme

Making excuses instead of giving reasons. Children (and adults) should differentiate between excuses and reasons.

Starters

Teacher: You may prefer to frame questions that are more relevant to your own school situation.

1 Who got up late this morning?

2 Who did not do their homework last night?

3 Who is not wearing correct school uniform today?

4 Who didn't bring their (PE/football/netball/swimming) kit today?

5 Who promised to (walk the dog/feed the cat/goldfish/budgie etc) last night and did not?

6 Who promised to wash up after dinner last night and did not?

7 Who did not clean their teeth this morning?

8 Who did not wash this morning (yes, really)?

You can probably think of many more …

Story

Seven sons and six excuses

Long ago, in a far-off land, there lived a High Prince, called Tuk Nah, who owned a herd of pure-white goats. One year, however, the precious goats began to disappear, one by one, one every night between sunset and sunrise. It was clear that a tiger was on the prowl.

Now the Prince had seven strong sons and he decided that they should be the ones to kill the tiger, because they could not help but be as brave as he was himself. Yet, after three days of hunting in the jungle, where they made a great deal of noise and probably gave the tiger nothing worse than a headache, they returned to the palace, empty-handed, to kneel in front of their father. He demanded that they explain their failure to kill the tiger.

The six eldest sons had ready excuses for their lack of success – a broken bow-string, a bent spear, a disturbed ants' nest, an angry snake, an interfering monkey and a rampaging elephant were all held to blame. Tuk Nah listened to the string of excuses, his face being more displeased by the moment and his expression even more thunderous.

When he had listened to the six eldest he turned to his youngest son, Pham Ho, and said in a most sour voice, 'And what of you, youngest son? Bitten by a flea? Trodden on by a hare? Spat on by a lizard? Sword turned into butter? Come, come, I cannot wait to hear your excuse. For excuses are all I have heard until now and none of them reasons.'

'No, my father,' trembled Pham Ho, because his father was a fearsome man, 'None of these. I came face to face with the tiger in its lair. But when he opened his great mouth and I saw the size of his teeth, I was most afraid. So I ran away.'

The High Prince opened his eyes wide and burst into loud peals of laughter so much as to make him cry. When his merriment had subsided, he said, between his tears, 'Take heed of this, all who are here present. My youngest son has not come up with an excuse for not killing the tiger but a good reason. And is not that one reason worth ten thousand excuses?' Then he said that Pham Ho was to be his heir and also made him a Great Lord to be going on with.

As for his six brothers, they were sent to work as goatherds until they discovered the difference between an excuse and a reason. I must tell you that it did not take them very long to find out.

The message is ...

Excuses are invented whereas reasons are not.

Songs

I listen and I listen	*Come & Praise* 60
Take the time to cogitate	*Every Colour* 47
Both sides now	*Alleluya* 33

A thought to share

Reasons are more likely to be believed than excuses because they are the truth.

Are you listening, God?

Lord, help us to realise that we should never do anything without a good reason.

Dear God, give us the courage to face up to the consequences of our actions.

Show us, Father God, how to make decisions and, if they are wrong, give us the strength to admit that they are.

21
Every little helps

Theme

Pollution by litter. Most schools pay great attention to the problem of litter but some extra emphasis is never wasted.

Starters

1 What is litter?
2 Are some kinds of litter worse than others?
3 In what ways can litter be disposed of?
4 What is pollution?
5 Is litter a kind of pollution?

The subject can be pursued in the classroom.

Story

The phantom cup

I'm not saying that I saw what happened with my own eyes nor am I sure that I believe it myself but you can make up your own mind. An ordinary sort of man, called Monty Notty, took his daughter, Amber, to the hospital because she had hurt her arm. After they had seen the doctor, Monty bought them each a drink from a machine. The drinks came in two plastic cups. Amber threw her empty cup in the bin, as most sensible people do, but her father threw his on the floor.

'Aren't you going to put that in the bin?' asked Amber. Monty laughed and said, 'No way,' and marched off to the car, not giving Amber time to pick up the cup. Then Monty saw the plastic cup on the shelf above the steering wheel. It had coffee stains inside it and it was quite warm. Monty opened the car window and threw the cup out.

'Very funny, Amber,' he snorted. His daughter started to protest that he had got into the car first but Monty was in no mood to listen.

They arrived home. And there, on the hall table, next to the telephone was .. a plastic cup with coffee-stains inside – and still warm. Monty yelled and threw it out of the nearest window. He did not see where it had landed, but, for the next twenty-four hours, wherever Monty went the cup appeared – in the bath, in his wardrobe, in his golf bag, on his office desk and on his computer keyboard. What made matters worse was that nobody else could see it and he thought he was going mad. It was when he found it in his car, once again, that he did the obvious thing – he got out of his car and … threw it into the nearest litter bin.

And that was the last he saw of it.

All right, so you think it is a silly story. Whoever heard of anyone being haunted by a plastic cup with coffee stains inside it? But I can't help wondering why Monty Notty resigned from his job as a computer programmer and got himself a job at a recycling works.

The message is ...

The only place for litter is in a bin.

Songs

Pollution calypso	*Every Colour* 16
Pollution	*Jolly Herring* 19
Milk bottle tops and paper bags	*Someone's Singing, Lord* 17

A thought to share

Someone must have ben the first person to dump litter.

Are you listening, God?

Lord of us all, teach us to care for our world.

Show us, dear God, give us the wisdom needed to fight pollution as best we can.

Father God, we shall have this day only once. Help us not to waste it

22
Two little words

Theme

Simple politeness in saying 'Thank you'. The phrase seems to be going out of fashion, especially with teenagers, although they are not alone.

Starters

1 Why do we say 'Thank you' when given something or when someone has done us a service?

2 Why do so many people say 'Cheers' and 'There you go' and other things instead of 'Thank you?'

3 Who thinks this is just as polite as saying 'Thank you'?

4 Does it matter?

Story

Two simple things

Many years ago, when much of the world was still a mystery, a small band of explorers was lost in the South American jungle. They wandered for days, unable to find their way out of the steaming, green darkness of the tall trees that almost shut out the light of the sun.

Then, one cold dawn, they woke from restless sleep to find they were surrounded by fierce warriors with faces painted in bright red stripes. These huge men were armed with fearsome spears and carried great shields made from leopard skins. The wanderers were herded through the jungle like so many goats until they came to mighty gates which led into a magnificent city in which the buildings, stretching as far as their eyes could see, were roofed with gold. Beyond the city they could see the sullen, smoking cone of a volcano.

The warriors forced them to bow to the volcano and then dragged the captives to a great gold palace. They were driven into an enormous hall in the palace and forced to kneel before the wizened old man who was sitting on a golden throne.

He spoke to them in their own language of Portugese, 'I am Mozana, king of the Almani. You have trespassed in my kingdom for which the penalty is death. Within three days, you shall be fed to Sharla, our fiery mountain god. But you could escape this terrible punishment by giving me two simple things. They will cost you nothing but are most precious to me, as they should be to you. Take them away.' The trembling men were hauled to their feet and thrown into a dark cave.

On the following day, the explorers knelt before Mozana again. 'Have you decided what are the two simple things that I want from you?' he asked. In turn, each explorer offered the king two of their most cherished belongings.

Don Pasquale offered the king a pair of fine Toledo swords, studded with diamonds and worth a fortune. The priest, Father Manuel, would have parted with his two precious prayer books. Each prisoner tried to please the king with jewels, gold coins, cloaks and shoes.

But, to each offering, the king shook his head and said in his tremulous voice, 'I do not want your riches or possessions, whether in twos or not.'

He turned his attention to Julio da Silva, the youngest member of the party, only sixteen and but a helper to the cook.

'You have offered me nothing so far, young man,' he said, smiling sadly, 'Can you not tell me what I want from you that costs nothing but is worth everything?'

Although terrified, the boy looked Mozana straight in the eye, saying boldly, 'Lord, I have nothing to give but the two words, 'Thank you' if you should spare my life. These words cost nothing but mean everything to me because they could save my life.'

Shakily, and with the assistance of two attendants, the king stood up and cried, 'This is the only wise man in your number although he is of tender years! He has shown us all that simple gratitude in the shape of the two words 'Thank you' is worth more than any treasure. These two words were the precious things that I sought from you!

I am well pleased. Now leave me. You are all free to go.'

The explorers were led from the city, laden with precious gifts and food and water, eventually to find their way back to civilisation.

Julio de Silva is an old man now but still tells this tale to any one who will listen and says 'Thank you' when the story has been told.

The message is ...

Saying 'Thank you' takes no effort but it means a great deal to those who are thanked.

Songs

A living song	*Come & Praise* 72
Thank you for my friends	*Tinderbox* 31
Stand up, clap hands	*Someone's Singing, Lord* 14

A thought to share

What do 'Cheers' and 'There you go' really mean?

Are you listening, God?

Lord, teach us to thank others when they do us a kindness or make us a gift.

Dear God, let us never be ashamed to express our thanks when we are grateful.

Thank you, Father God, for all your good gifts to us.

23
Get rid of the water wings

Theme

The importance of being able to swim. All children should be encouraged to learn to swim well enough to survive in case of emergency.

Starters

1 Who can swim properly?
2 Who is learning to swim?
3 Should everyone learn to swim? Why?

Story

The day Icarus got wet

The old Greek myth tells us that the first man to fly was Icarus. He flew with a pair of wings made from feathers and wax. The myth also tells us that he flew too near the sun, the wax melted, the wings fell apart and he crashed into the sea. But I have heard another version. He did fly, using a pair of wings made by his father.

Daedalus was a clever man who worked for King Minos of Crete, an island in the Mediterranean Sea. Some of you may have been there on holiday. According to the Greek story, Daedalus had an argument with the King and decided to fly out of Crete before Minos fed him to a rather unpleasant creature, half-man and half-bull, called the Minotaur.

Icarus, however, saw the wings in his father's workshop and decided that he wanted to be the first to try them out. Daedalus, however, would not let his son try them out because there was only one place to test them. That was over the sea and Icarus could not ... swim. He would not even learn. He even refused to get his big toe wet. So his father was taking no chances.

Yet Icarus was so determined that he crept into his father's workshop, early one morning, and helped himself. He strapped on the wings and ran along the beach as fast as he could, flapping the wings with all his might and main. To his astonishment he went soaring into the air.

A small crowd of his friends who had come down to the beach for a morning swim watched him as he hurtled over the waves, swooping and diving and climbing high into the bright blue sky. Down he came again, skimming the waves, shouting with excitement. Then he flew too low, the tip of a wing hit the sea, it fell to bits and Icarus plummeted into the warm, blue Aegean sea. There he splashed and thrashed and spluttered and flailed about in the water, calling for help but all to no avail. Poor Icarus disappeared under the waves before anyone could reach him.

And you don't have to be clever to work out what happened to him.

The message is ...

A life might depend on being able to swim – and it could be yours.

Songs

It's a new day	*Come & Praise* 106
There's so much pleasure	*Every Colour* 10
For all the strength	*Someone's Singing, Lord* 16

A thought to share

If we need wings to fly why don't we need flippers to swim?

Are you listening, God?

Thank you, Lord, for swimming pools and for those who teach us how to swim.

Father God, teach us to be sensible children who take no risks in or near deep water, whether we can swim or not.

For our wonderful bodies and the chance to enjoy all sport and exercise, we thank you, God.

24
All together now!

Theme

Co-operation. In school, as in the wider world, there are times when children benefit from acting and working together.

Starters

Teacher: Refer to any great historical engineering project – it could be the pyramids or anything with which children may have some familiarity. In these Starters, Stonehenge is used as an example.

1 Who knows anything about Stonehenge?
2 How could men build such a massive structure without machinery?

Story

Gulliver's Travels
This story is paraphrased from Gulliver's Travels *by Dean Jonathan Swift, written in 1726.*

The ship's doctor staggered ashore, completely exhausted, and fell asleep on the soft, short grass. He knew not how long he lay there, but when he tried to get up, he found that he could not move. His arms, legs, body and hair were securely fastened to the ground.

Something seemed to be crawling on his chest. He looked down and, to his astonishment, the prisoner realised he was looking at a tiny human being, no more than 15 centimetres tall. Soon more than forty creatures, of similar proportions, were walking on his body.

The castaway was amazed by the scene and his predicament and infuriated by his restraint. Nevertheless, he could only marvel at the incredible teamwork that had brought about his present situation. The reluctant visitor then became so angry at the thought of being overcome by such puny manikins that he began to roar and to struggle. He managed to release one arm and to loosen his head.

But before he could grab any of the tiny people, he heard a cry in a shrill little voice, 'Tolgo phonac!' and immediately felt as if his face and hands had been pricked by a thousand sharp needles. His miniature captors had fired a shower of arrows into the air so as to land vertically upon him. Meanwhile, others were attempting to stick spears into his side, through his thick waistcoat, but without success.

It was not long, however, before the little persons were assured that the Man-Mountain – Quinbis Flestrin, as they called him in their language, meant them no harm. They dressed his tiny arrow-wounds and gave him food and drink and, later still, they became firm friends. Time passed and then, one day, he found a boat that had been washed up on the beach. The little people helped him to make sails and oars and gave him provisions. After a while, he was picked up by a big ship and found his way home.

Some time later, he described these adventures and others in a book. His name, if you have not guessed it already, was Gulliver and the land of the tiny people was Lilliput.

The message is ...

Although Gulliver was twelve times bigger than the Lilliputians, they made him their prisoner because they worked together as a team – they co-operated.

Songs

One more step	*Come & Praise* 72
Such hard work	*Every Colour* 29
Side by side	*Ta-ra-ra-boom-de-ay* 36

A thought to share

It is better to work with people than to work against them.

Are you listening, God?

Help us, Father, to work together for the good of everybody.

Father God, teach us that co-operation does not mean that we expect others to do our share of the work.

Dear God, please bless our school, so that by working together and playing together we may do our best at all times.

━━━━━━ HOME AND AWAY ━━━━━━

25
Being in control

Theme

Cycling safely (and using other 'wheels'). Although children may wear crash helmets and have gained proficiency certificates they must still exercise responsibility when using public thoroughfares.

Starters

1 Who uses a bicycle?
2 Who wears a crash helmet and other protective clothing?
3 Who has passed a Cycling Proficiency Test?
4 Does this guarantee that you are safe to cycle anywhere?
5 Who thinks it is a good idea to cycle on a footpath?
6 When it is not a good idea to do so?

Story

This story is paraphrased from an episode in The Willows in Winter *by William Horwood, in which are related the further adventures of the characters from* The Wind in the Willows *by Kenneth Grahame – especially the famous Toad of Toad Hall.*

Toad and an aeroplane

After his latest escape from prison and his adventures with the law, Toad was leading a quiet life, supervised by his friends. But, from the day that he saw the magical red and yellow aeroplane, he was doomed to return to his wild ways.

Secretly, he bought one of the latest flying machines and hired a man who would teach Toad to fly the contraption and to look after it. All would have been well, if Toad had not taken it into his giddy head that he could pilot the machine after only one lesson. Even worse, he took with him, on his first solo flight, an unwitting passenger, one terrified Rat.

Poor Ratty had absolutely no idea, when they first left solid earth, that the pilot was Toad. Toad the Showman, Toad the Foolhardy, Toad the Totally Untrained. This is not to say that dear Rat was a fool, but Toad's features and physique were so encumbered with the paraphernalia of pilotry that no one could identify the foolhardy animal.

The flight that followed was of such nightmare dimensions that Rat will never talk about it. It was only by sheer good fortune that Rat was able to descend to the ground with the aid of the new-fangled invention called a parachute. Toad, however, continued his erratic aerial voyage, full of his own importance, singing his own praises, and generally being an aerial clown, convinced that an admiring crowd was watching below, amazed by his marvellous aerobatics. What the foolish animal seemed not to understand was that the aircraft was, in fact, flying itself and that his swoops and dives and loops were more a result of air currents than his skill, which, in truth, did not exist.

Small wonder, then that, after a period of time had elapsed in which Toad persuaded himself that he was truly an intrepid aviator, the machine ran out of petrol and hit the ground sufficiently hard enough to break into a thousand pieces of wood and a million tatters of fabric. The dashing pilot, meanwhile, had managed to escape by parachute, like Rat, before the aeroplane crashed and ended up crashing through, and dangling from, the roof of a glass greenhouse.

Despite all this, Toad, still considered himself a hero and went on to begin another series of his hair-raising escapades.

The message is ...

People using vehicles should have total control of them at all times.

Songs

Travel on	*Come & Praise* 42
Wheels keep turning	*Apusskidu* 24
Roller skating	*Harlequin* 23

A thought to share

There is an old saying about riding a bicycle with no hands on the handlebars – no hands, no head.

Are you listening, God?

Keep us safe, Lord, when we are enjoying ourselves on wheels and help us to remember that we are not the only travellers.

Thank you, God, for bicycles, skateboards, roller skates and roller-blades. Give us the wisdom to use them sensibly and safely.

Father God, give good sense and good manners to all those who travel by road.

26
Eating seriously *

Theme

Over-indulgence in food. Many children not only over-eat but they eat the wrong things. So do many adults.

Teacher: Approach the topic with caution, being aware of your own school population. If you wish to avoid controversy, discuss 'healthy eating' and read the poem at your own risk.

Starters

1 Suggest some reasons why people eat (necessity? enjoyment?).
2 Do some people eat more than they need? Why?
3 What are the dangers of not eating enough of the right kind of food?

You may prefer to follow up, from here on, in the classroom.

4 Is drinking of soft drinks just as undesirable?
5 Does it matter if some people weigh more than others of the same size and age?

or

4 Do we eat too much of the wrong kind of food?
5 What is the wrong kind of food? Why?

Poem

The Sad Tale of Elsie Rita, who was Far Too Fond of Eating

A girl by name of Elsie Rita
Denied she was an over-eater,
Her parents begged her not to risk it
By eating sixteen chocolate biscuits.
Young Elsie said, 'I won't be told
To give up ice cream and Swiss roll.
Eat not to live but live to eat
All kinds of savoury and sweet,
Crisps and pickles, pizza, ham,
Hot kebabs and curried lamb,
Sweet and sour, thick crisp batter,
Pile it up, it doesn't matter.
How I worship chips and fish
Making mountains on a dish.
Italian, Chinese, Indian food,
Who cares? I think it does me good!

I don't agree that I am greedy –
It's just my appetite that's needy.'
The years went by and Elsie ate
And ate and ate all she could get.
But, after eating twelve fried eggs,
She lost the power of her legs.
Her parents had to hire a crane
To get her vertical again.
Her father cried, 'She has to diet!'
But Elsie said, 'I must deny it.'
The doctor said, in warning voice,
'Come, come, young lady, you've no choice.
Whether you lie or sit or stand,
For you all kinds of food are banned.'
Poor Elsie uttered dreadful shrieks
But had to starve for two whole weeks.
The kilos melted right away
And by the following Saturday
The doctor said how well she'd done
And now the girl could have some fun.
Delighted that she'd lost some weight
She had a feast to celebrate,
At which she soon resumed the habit
And ate a pie of Chinese rabbit.
No sooner was her stomach loaded
Than Elsie, with a bang, exploded!
Her mother wailed, 'I knew she'd pop,
She never knew when she should stop.'
Now, children, learn from Elsie's fate,
Control your diet – and your weight.

The message is ...

Nobody has ever exploded from over-eating but you do your body no
favours by over-filling it with food.

Songs

Bread for the world   *Come & Praise* 73
The hungry man   *Every Colour* 47
When a dinosaur's feeling hungry   *Tinderbox* 12

A thought to share

The time to stop eating is when you think you can eat a little more.

Are you listening, God?

Teach us, Lord, the difference between need and greed.

Father God, remind us now and again that we eat to live and not live to eat.

Dear God, thank you for our food. Let us never waste it or abuse it but be grateful that we have it.

27
It must be true

Theme

Gullibility and advertising. Children are very susceptible to the persuasive powers of TV advertising.

Starters

1 Who has ever bought anything because they saw it in a TV commercial?
2 Did you make the right decision?
3 If you had seen the product advertised in a magazine, would you have bought it?
4 If the product had not been advertised at all, would you have bought it?
5 Do you think advertisers always tell the truth about their products?

Story

The miracle brew

The small crowd gathered around the gaily-painted wagon, listening to the black-bearded 'medicine man'. He held up a bottle of a bright red liquid and smacked it.

'Now lookee here, folks,' he invited them, 'I have just got tell you that you are looking at the marvel of the nineteenth century. You see here in my hand' – he smacked the bottle again – 'the wonder of this year of our Lord, eighteen hundred and eighty five.'

A woman, her face sharp enough to freeze vinegar, demanded, in a shrill voice, 'You never mind all them high-falutin' words, Mister, just you all tell us what that stuff does. And how much it costs. Mighty pricey, I'll be bound.' The small crowd guffawed and the medicine man took off his tall, black hat, shaking his head with mock despair.

'Why, Ma'am, ain't it the secret Pawnee Injun cure for just about everythin' from snakebite to sore feet. Drink it or you can rub it on, miracles is guaranteed. And only a dollar a bottle. Or you can have two bottles for a dollar ninety-five.'

A red-faced cowboy bellowed, 'I bet it don't cure saddle-sores none!'

'Sir,' laughed the medicine man, 'Just rub it on the afflicted parts and drink half a bottle of whiskey afterwards. I will guarantee you will feel no pain!' The small crowd hooted with laughter.

'It don't cure bellyache,' called out a little old man at the edge of the crowd.

The salesman snapped, 'You have my word, Mister, that our President Grover Cleveland was cured of a feverish appendix after just one spoonful of this here medicine.'

The old man pulled out an ancient revolver and the crowd scattered in all directions.

He announced. 'Your brew didn't cure my wife. In fact, it killed her, according to the doctor in Yellowstone Gulch. Which just goes to show you can't believe everything that a salesman tells you.'

Then he pointed the old gun at the medicine-man and shot him, right through his tall hat. I reckon the salesman is still a-runnin'…

The message is ….

It is unwise to accept all the claims made for products, in advertisements, without question.

Songs

Both sides now	*Alleluya* 33
Take the time to cogitate	*Every Colour* 47
Give to us eyes	*Someone's Singing, Lord* 18

A thought to share

If 'new and improved' detergent now washes whiter than ever, what was wrong with it before?

Are you listening, God?

Father, help us to understand that the purpose of an advertisement is to sell something.

Lord, teach us not to be hasty people, but to think before we act.

Give us, Father God, the wisdom to know which is fact and which is exaggeration.

28
A place for everything

Theme

Order is preferable to chaos. Many people are untidy but they can still make life easier by trying to be more orderly.

Starters

1 Who couldn't find their dinner money/football boots/PE kit before school today? Why?
2 Who puts things away in a 'safe' place and can never find them when they are wanted?
3 Who thinks untidiness doesn't matter? Why?

Story

This story is an imaginary extract from a non-existent, undiscovered manuscript that Lewis Carroll never wrote.

Alice finds another tea party

Alice found herself in front of a small cottage. To her eyes it closely resembled a cricket pavilion. The December Hare, who looked exactly like Santa Claus, except for his long ears, was ironing a sleeping hedgehog, without success, because its prickles refused to lie flat. She looked across the lawn at a person dressed in white and wearing a blue top hat.

'Just be sure to iron my cricket pads,' he said as he bowled an imaginary cricket ball at the Hare.

'You must be the Mad Batter,' said Alice, brightly, curtseying to the odd figure.

'Indeed I am,' he warbled, 'As the tenth innings is now over, it has to be teatime. Again.' He said sharply to the Hare, 'Serve tea.' The Hare picked up the gigantic yellow watering-can on the table and poured milk into two enormous cups, spilling torrents of milk on to the tablecloth in the process.

'Have a chocolate biscuit!' carolled the Mad Batter, taking the lid off a saucepan, only to replace it hurriedly as a thunderous snore echoed from inside.

'Ah, none left,' he trilled, waving a hand delicately, 'What a pity.'

The Mad Batter picked up a flower pot and asked Alice, 'Would you care for a cucumber sandwich? One should always eat cucumber sandwiches at cricket matches, you know.' He looked into the flower-pot. 'Oh, my gracious goodness, it has a hole in the bottom. No sandwiches, I am afraid. Still, it is Friday.'

Alice decided that it was time to ask a question so she enquired politely, 'Please, why do you keep things in such strange containers?'

The Mad Batter looked quite offended as he spooned sugar out of a goldfish bowl, using a garden trowel, into one of the cups of milk.

'Strange, child, strange?' he carolled, 'There is nothing strange about them. I know where everything is.' He pointed with a handy cricket stump at the December Hare, who was trying to get jam out of a china piggy-bank with a knife blade. 'And so does he, most of the time. Why, we have a place for everything and everything in its place.

Now it is time for the next innings. Would you care to umpire?' he asked, with a huge smile.

At which point, Alice decided that indeed, enough was enough and she ran off down a passage that had just appeared in a convenient oak tree.

The message is...

Life can be easier if you have a place for everything.

Songs

A living song	*Come & Praise* 72
Working together	*Every Colour* 37
One, two, three	*Tinderbox* 65

A thought to share

Have a place for everything but remember where the place is.

Are you listening, God?

Lord, help us to think clearly and to act sensibly.

Father God, give us willing hands so that we may help others unselfishly.

Teach us, good Lord, to be people upon whom others can depend.

29
A bad master*

Theme

Fire risks. It is not just toddlers who play with combustible materials. Many schools have a programme of inculcating fire-risk awareness and involve the services of friendly firefighters.

Teacher: Some children have a deep-seated fear of fire and it is prudent not to over-dramatise the topic.

Starters

1 What are the main causes of fires at home? (smoking materials, kitchen accidents, electrical faults)
2 What can children do to reduce the risks of fires starting?
3 What are two things that children should not do if they discover a fire? (try to extinguish it; panic)
4 What should children do if fire is discovered (a) at school (b) at home (c) anywhere else?

Story

The Bringing of fire

The old Viking warrior threw his pork-bone into the roaring flames.

'Grandfather,' asked little Aelfred, 'How did we get fire into our land without getting burnt?'

Harald told him, 'Oh, for that we must thank a brave Norse jarl, or lord, called Erif. When he lived, the world was cold and covered with ice and snow and no one in the world knew about fire. One day, Erif set off on a voyage to Iceland to look for whales. But a mighty storm swept the whole crew overboard, and the longboat drifted helplessly towards a black shore, with only Erif left on board.

As dawn broke, Erif found himself on a black shore backed by towering cliffs. He scaled them and, when he reached the top, saw, stretching in front of him as far as his eyes could see, pillars of flame that leapt up from the ground and died away, only to burst every now and then into life. Now Erif had never seen fire before, so he could not know whether these flames were hot or cold. Yet, strangely, they had no heat in them at all.

He ran towards the fiery pillars and picked one up as it was dwindling, meaning to put it into the leather pouch on his belt. But, as he was about to do so, the little flame changed into a fierce, orange dragon.

'Thou shouldst not be here in this sacred place, puny mortal,' roared the dragon. 'Only the great gods are allowed to walk here. For your impudence, I shall eat you.'

Erif, although greatly frightened, would not show his fear and answered boldly, 'I mean no harm. I was cast on the black shore after crossing the sea. What is thy name? Mine is Erif.' No sooner had he spoken his name than the fearsome dragon shrank until it was no bigger than Erif's foot.

In a tiny voice, it begged his forgiveness, saying, 'O thou of the magic name, take away what thou will.'

I know not how Erif managed to get home again but he did, and brought the flame with him. And, when he opened the door of the Great Hall, the tiny pillar of flame jumped out of the pouch and on to the floor and it became hot. He threw sticks on to it and so was made the first fire. This, my grandson, is the story of how fire came to the cold lands of the far north before it came to any other. And, if you think about it, you will easily work out why Erif had a name magic enough to tame the fire-dragon.'

The message is ...

There isn't, really ... the significance of the assembly should emerge from the Starters and any ensuing discussion.

Songs

In the bustle of the city	*Come & Praise* 101
Look around	*Every Colour* 9
The fireman	*Apusskidu* 33

A thought to share

A fire is easier to light than it is to put out.

Are you listening, God?

Father of us all, give us the wisdom to recognise that fire is dangerous.

Lord, give us good sense where fire is concerned and never let us forget what damage it can do.

Dear God, protect and care for brave firefighters who may have to pay a terrible price for other people's stupidity.

━━━━ THAT'S LIFE! ━━━━

30
Saying 'Sorry' seriously

Theme

Apologising meaningfully. Insincere apologies are better left unsaid.

Starters

1 What words are used to apologise?
2 What is important about making an apology? (sincerity)
3 Should you offer any more than an apology if you have offended a
   person in some way? (making amends)

Story

The well-mannered Empress

Many years ago, a far-off eastern land was ruled by a cruel Empress,
who insisted that all her subjects were required to be polite to one
another at all times. If someone trod on another's toes an apology had
to be made, perhaps 'I am so sorry' or 'Please forgive me, I am so
clumsy. Perhaps you would like to sit down for a moment while I fetch
you some refreshment?'

Such apologies had to be made in every case of offence, real or
imaginary. Failure to do so meant arrest by the Polite Police who were
very sorry but you had to be taken before the Polite Judge who would
beg your pardon before sending you to the salt mines for ten years.

If one committed a serious crime, such as theft, the accused was
always tried by the Empress herself. She always found the accused,
'Guilty' and always sentenced him or her to have their head cut off.
Mind you, the Empress always apologised for her verdict and the
sentence. One day alone, she sentenced to death a baker, who had sold
a loaf that was too light and a farmer's wife for selling bad eggs. Of

course, she apologised to them both. Then a small girl was led in, chained hand and foot.

'Hah! A child criminal!' screamed the Empress. 'The worst kind of all! You must say 'Sorry' to the fruit farmer for stealing two cherries from his orchard. And please accept my sincere apologies but you must have your head chopped off. Take her away!' But the little girl refused to go. She stamped her feet and hung on to the dock.

Shaking her chains at the Empress, she screamed, 'Yes, I am sorry that I stole the cherries. It was quite wrong of me and I will mean it when I apologise to the farmer. But your apologies to me do not mean anything. So why bother to say them at all?'

The Empress was so astonished that she ordered the girl's release and, from that day on, she never apologised to anyone again for sentencing them to death. Mind you, they lost their heads anyway. I suppose that is more honest, but small consolation if you and your head are parted.

The message is ...

When you apologise you are really saying, 'I won't do it again.'

Songs

You've got to move	*Come & Praise* 72
Seeds of kindness	*Every Colour* 42
Love somebody	*Tinderbox* 16

A thought to share

If you don't like apologising don't upset anyone.

Are you listening, God?

Dear God, teach us to do what is right but, if we do wrong, help us to say that we are sorry.

Help us to remember, Lord, that apologising is not a sign of weakness.

Father God, forgive us
For the things we have done wrong,
For bad temper and angry words,
For selfishness and greed,
For making others unhappy,
Forgive us, Father God.

31
Who's afraid of what?

Theme

Fears. It is a rare individual, child or adult, who has no fears, sometimes becoming phobias. Probably the most common fear of all is that of the unknown or the unfamiliar.

Starters

Teacher: If you are brave enough to confess to your own personal fears, this can create a positive atmosphere. At the same time, don't overdo it …

1 Who is brave enough to tell us of their real fears? (no invention wanted)

2 How can we stand up to our fears, even if only for the time being? (whistling, singing, cuddling &c)

3 Who knows, without mentioning any names, of adults who have real fears?

Story

The roaring mouse

Erica is an average sort of elephant, living in a Zoo. One hot day, she was just about to flop down in the corner and have a little nap when she saw … it. It was a creature unlike anything she had ever seen before – small and furry, with a long pink tail and twitchy whiskers. Yes, a mouse. Erica had never, ever seen a mouse before and she was terrified.

The mouse stood up on its hind legs, making fists with its tiny paws and squeaked ferociously, 'Wanna fight, Dumbo? Come on, then, big nose, come on, come on!'

Erica cowered in her corner and trumpeted, 'Oh please don't hurt me.'

The mouse stopped waving his fists, put his paws on his hips and scratched his head, looking puzzled.

'Say, Trunky, you really are chicken, aren't you?' he squeaked.

'I'm not a chicken,' said Erica, sounded offended, 'I'm an elephant. But what are you?'

The mouse puffed out his chest and sneered, 'I'm a mouse, stupid. And I should be scared of you. Mice should be scared of elephants. Not the other way round.'

Erica thought for a flapping her floppy ears and swaying her trunk gently. Then she said thoughtfully, 'Do you know, mouse, you are absolutely right. So they should.' And with that, she raised her great foot and made as if to stamp on the mouse. But when her foot was just a millimetre above the quivering little creature, Erica said with a little elephant giggle, 'Oh, I can't do this. I may not be scared of you. But I think you're rather sweet, really. Now clear off.'

The mouse could not believe his ears. Not at being told to the 'Clear off' – but being described as sweet.

He hoped none of his pals were listening – he'd never live it down.

The message is ...

It is rather silly being afraid of something if you don't know what there is to be afraid of.

Songs

When a knight won his spurs	*Come & Praise* 50
I can climb	*Every Colour* 17
I whistle a happy tune	*Apusskidu* 3

A thought to share

Only fools go into battle with no fear.

Are you listening, God?

Father, give us strength to face our fears, whatever they may be.

Lord, be with those people who have real reasons to be afraid – those who are living through war and famine and all that is evil.

Father God, when we are truly scared by things we see and hear, help us to remember that You are always with us and that need we have no fear.

32
Softly, softly

Theme

Persuasion is the most effective way of getting something done. The old story of the Wind and the Sun bears re-telling, but the story below is a different version, albeit with a twist.

Starter

Which of these methods are the best way of getting someone to do something for you :-

threats?	bribes?
begging?	giving reasons?
sulking,	crying?

What reasons would you give for your choice?

Story

The best way

A farmer by the name of Obadiah Clomp was making his weekly journey to market, his cart loaded with vegetables. As he passed Crown Wood, Jack Stamp the highwayman leapt out, waving a pistol.

'Stand and deliver!' shouted the highwayman,

'I've got no money,' grinned Obadiah, 'But you can have a turnip.' With that, he threw his biggest turnip at Jack, hitting him on the head. Jack was not expecting this, so he ran away. When Obadiah reached the next milestone, old Billy Topp was standing there, holding out a metal cup.

'Spare us a coin, Mister,' whined old Billy, 'I'm starving and my house has burnt down.'

'Your fine boots tell me that you are no more starving than I am,' laughed Obadiah, 'But here, this will make you cry all the better.' With that, he threw his biggest onion at old Billy, hitting him on the nose so that he ran down the road, howling.

At the next milestone stood a monk in a brown habit. He smiled warmly at Obadiah and said, 'My son, all our crops have been spoilt by floods and all the monks are very hungry. Could I ask you to bring your cartload of vegetables to the monastery so that my brothers may have a decent meal? It would be so kind of you and you will be thrice blessed in our prayers.'

Obadiah stroked his chin and said, thoughtfully, 'You ask a lot, Father. But, whereas I do not take threats nor accept lies I can be persuaded by soft words. Show me the way to the monastery because I need my horse and cart to get home.'

All the monks sang psalms of praise when Obadiah arrived with his welcome load. They said prayers for him and his family and the Abbot, who was the Head Monk, laid hands upon the farmer's head and blessed him.

Obadiah said, however, 'I am grateful for your prayers and am even more convinced that soft words are more persuasive than threats. But my dear wife will not appreciate my giving away all our vegetables and she will expect me to have received some payment for them.'

He appeared so distressed by this idea, that the Abbott paid him three shillings for the vegetables, which seemed to satisfy everyone. Even Obadiah's wife. And she was not easy to persuade.

The message is ...

Persuasion probably requires more patience but it is worth it in the end.

Songs

I come like a beggar	*Come & Praise* 90
Seeds of kindness	*Every Colour* 42
With a little help from my friends	*Alleluya* 38

A thought to share

There are many ways of persuading people to do what you would like them to, but using force or lying are not the best ways.

Are you listening, God?

Lord, teach us that violence is not the answer to most problems.

Father God, help us to understand that there are more ways than one of solving a problem.

Show us, dear God, that we cannot always get our own way in everything.

33
What is beautiful?

Theme

Beauty is a subjective concept. The old adage that says, 'Beauty is in the eye of the beholder' is still valid, whether it refers to physical appearance, artifacts, natural phenomena, clothing and so on.

Starters
** = *any contemporary pop group/football team/or whatever*

1   Who thinks ** is/are the greatest? (Management of responses will require discretion …!)
2   Having established a majority view, ask why?
3   Do the same for a minority view and ask why?

This can be discussed profitably in the classroom and can be useful for statistical work. But then, you have probably done that already …

Story

Space opinions

Space-Courier Kee sipped her drink and continued, 'There I was, light years away from base and all I could see was this boring desert of grey dust, mile after mile of it. I set my emergency beacon and went outside the shuttle while I waited for the Space Association recovery to arrive. I had only taken two steps outside the airlock when I saw the thing, barely five metres away. And the smell, oh, if I hadn't smelt it for myself I wouldn't have believed it. It was just foul. The alien itself was no more than a disgusting, wobbly, slimy orange blob. It reminded me of a slug like you'd get on Earth but hundreds of times bigger.

I wasn't prepared, though, I can tell you, for it to speak to me – in English.

'Ship broken down? So has mine,' it said politely in a wobbly, slimy sort of voice. It wobbled like a massive orange jelly and went on, 'Pray excuse my being so blunt, but where have you come from?'

Before I could answer, the blob said, 'I must ask because you must be the ugliest creature on which I have ever clapped eyes.'

I thought, looking at its twenty eyes, each one of which resembled a fried egg, 'What a cheek,' but restrained myself and said, 'I beg your pardon. I come from the third planet in the Sol galaxy. I am a human. A Terran. An Earth dweller.'

Blob made a noise that sounded a bit like someone being sick and said, 'Are they all as revolting as you are?'

I thought that was a bit over the top and said, seriously annoyed by now, 'You must be joking. You are the most disgusting-looking thing I have ever seen in all my travels.'

The horrible lump rolled around in a jelly-like ball, making the most deafening, squealing noises. Then it stopped abruptly and changed colour. But, before it could say anything else, we both heard another voice. Hovering behind Blob was a shimmering, ghostly shape, almost transparent.

It spoke softly, almost in a whisper, 'Beauty means different things to different people. What is ugliness to one is beauty to another. So stop arguing, go home and leave me in peace on this beautiful planet.'

I was going to say something about this awful place then I realised what the shape had said. It's quite true when you think about it, isn't it?'

The message is ...

Everybody has their own idea of what is beautiful and what is not.

Songs

All things bright and beautiful	*Come & Praise* 3
Points of View	*Every Colour* 45
God created them all	*Songs for Every Day* 54

A thought to share

Do you think the person you love most in the world is beautiful?

Are you listening, God?

Lord of the Universe, help us to understand that all people do not think alike.

Father God, teach us to respect the views of others and to recognise that we are not always right.

Father of us all, give us the wisdom to appreciate that everything is beautiful in its own way.

34
The corporal in waiting

Theme

Keeping promises. People make promises, sometimes meaning to keep them and sometimes not.

Starters

1 Who has been promised something and then been let down? Why?
2 Who has ever made a promise, meaning to keep it and then breaking it? Why?
3 Who has ever made a promise with no intention of keeping it? Why?
4 Should we do our best to keep promises even if we regret making them in the first place?

Story

This story is based on a true incident.

The loyal corporal

The US Navy launch crunched ashore on the white sand of the apparently deserted island, a mere speck in the vastness of the Pacific Ocean. The first Marine jumped over the side and wandered up the gently-sloping beach.

Ten seconds later he was running for his life as a hail of machine-gun bullets kicked up the sand around his feet. He flung himself into the boat and panted, 'Get us out of here, man!' and the coxswain in charge of the launch needed no urging.

Dawn was approaching as a bigger party, in battle order, crawled up the beach as other Marines might have done twenty years before. They crept towards the tumble-down hut in the trees, Lieutenant Webb keeping an eye on the machine-gun he could see poking out through the sandbags in front of the hut. He sidled as quietly as he could into the dimness of the hut. In the gloom he could see a man on a bed, sleeping. Lieutenant Webb stuck his gun into the man's ribs. With a startled yelp, the sleeper sat up. The Marines could not believe their eyes. Their enemy was a little grey-bearded old man, wearing a tattered khaki uniform with two stripes on the left sleeve.

Corporal Hoto, of the Imperial Japanese Army been waiting for the invasion since 1944, not knowing that Japan had surrendered in 1945. His platoon of twenty men had volunteered to stay on the island and defend it to the death after the main garrison had left to fight in Okinawa. Colonel Yui had given him his own sword and promised him that he would return after Japan's victory.

Hoto was not to know that the Colonel and his men had died two hours after leaving the island, when their ship was torpedoed by a submarine. No ship came near the island for the next twenty-one years. There was no radio and the small band of soldiers had died, one by one, from sharks, poisonous fish and disease, leaving Hoto all alone for eight long years, still waiting for the Americans.

But, as the little Corporal said to his grandchildren when he returned home to Tokyo, 'The Colonel made me a promise. It was not his fault that he did not keep it.' And Hoto would blame no one.

The message is ...

Some people will go to any lengths to keep a promise, but there are times when one has to be realistic.

Songs

You shall go out with joy	Come & Praise 98
Do your best	Every Colour 48
Love somebody	Tinderbox 16

A thought to share

Jonathan Swift, the author of *Gulliver's Travels*, said that 'Promises and pie-crust are made to be broken'.

Are you listening, God?

Help us, Father God, not to make promises that we know we are unlikely to keep.

Dear God, teach us that breaking promises deliberately can cause unhappiness. Make us strong enough to do all we can to keep our promises.

Lord, teach us that broken promises can sometimes mean broken friendships.

35
Emergency! Emergency!

Theme

Reminding children of the way of summoning help in an emergency. Most children know about '999' but some memory-jogging is worthwhile.

Starters

1 Name the emergency services.
2 How do you call the emergency services if necessary?

Story

What an emergency!

Mrs Florrie Flapper had just returned from shopping. She walked up her front drive, looking forward to a cup of coffee. Then, to her horror, she saw a pair of legs sticking out from underneath the car. They were not moving.

'Bert,' she said sharply, 'Stop fooling around and come indoors for your coffee.' There was no reply. Florrie kicked one of the legs. Nothing happened. She kicked the other one. Still no sign of life.

Florrie tried to look under the car but she was, how shall I put it, a little too plump to do so. She screamed at the legs. They made no reply.

And what did she do?

She panicked. Mrs Flapper threw her shopping bag up in the air, ran up and down the drive, ran over the lawn and Bert's best petunias. She hammered on the bonnet of the car, kicked the wheels, shrieked and generally made an exhibition of herself.

Then she ran out into the road, yelling, 'Oh, my Bertie is dead, run over by his own car. What shall I do, what shall I do? Help! Help!'

Windows and doors opened all along the street as neighbours wondered what the commotion was about. Everyone stared at Florrie but no one moved a muscle to help her. It took nine-year old Katrina

Karm to stop the panic. She was trotting past on her way to buy sweets when she heard the dreadful noise that Mrs. Flapper was making. She did what any sensible person would do – she went into the nearest telephone kiosk and dialled '999'.

When asked what service she required, she said, calmly and clearly, 'Ambulance, please. A man at 45, Sunnyside seems to have been taken ill.'

This would have been a great story if Bert Flapper's life had been saved by Katrina's cool common sense. But there was nothing wrong with Bert. He had merely fallen asleep under his car when he was patching the exhaust. And Bert was a heavy sleeper. By the time the ambulance and the paramedics had arrived, he was standing by his car, wondering what all the fuss was about.

It took one young girl to know what to do. And you would do exactly the same … wouldn't you?

The message is …

In case of emergency, do not panic. But, whatever you do, do not call '999' unless there is a real emergency.

Songs

I was lying in the road	*Come & Praise* 88
Because you care	*Every Colour* 31
Love somebody	*Tinderbox* 16

A thought to share

Wanting to help somebody is little use if you don't know how.

Are you listening, God?

Father God, in case of danger give us the strength to keep calm.

Lord, during emergencies, give us clear heads and the ability to listen to those who know better than we do.

Dear God, thank you for the brave men and women of the emergency services who work without regard for their own safety.

36
Who needs legs? *

Theme

Overcoming physical disability. A brief account of the life and times of the late Douglas Bader, whose example inspired many limbless people to face up to and overcome their disabilities.

Teacher: You should, obviously, have regard to your own school population.

Starters

1   Does anyone know of anyone who has lost a limb?
2   Do they have problems? Or do they just not make them obvious?
3   Suggest things that people without limbs can do and do well.
4   What are the Paralympics?

Follow-up for classroom situations

1   How can life be made easier for disabled people, who, say, have to use wheelchairs?
2   Is this school designed to help people who do not find it easy to get around? How could it be improved?

If your commitments allow, it might be interesting to explore the topic further.

Narrative

Old tin legs

('Bader' is pronounced 'Barder'.)

Imagine, if you can, a small hospital ward in a French hospital, during the Second World War, more than fifty years ago.

A German officer clicks his heels and says, 'We have brought back your leg, Wing Commander Bader.' A soldier marches in and holds out a rigid arm, from which is suspended a leg. It is made of metal and it has been polished.

No, this is not a horror story nor is the leg real. It belongs to a Royal

Air Force pilot who has parachuted to earth after colliding with a German fighter aircraft during an air battle over France in 1941. Bader was to be a prisoner-of-war for the next four years, in one prison camp after another. The remarkable thing about Douglas Bader was not that he had only one leg – he had no legs at all.

His incredible story had begun ten years earlier. At the age of 21, he survived a horrific air crash that happened when he was doing low-flying stunts over an airfield near Reading in Berkshire. After many operations and a great deal of suffering, he left hospital with two metal legs instead of his own. From the first time that he strapped on his artificial legs, Douglas refused to use crutches or sticks, but, by sheer will power, he taught himself to walk.

Within a short space of time, he was back driving his beloved sports car. He even managed to pilot an Air Force aeroplane. He was, however, not allowed to take up flying duties again and he left the Air Force to work for a petroleum company. Bader got married, learned to dance, played golf and tennis and did most of the things that are done by people with two real legs.

When war came in 1939, he rejoined the RAF and became an ace fighter-pilot during the Battle of Britain in 1940 until he was shot down and captured. After the war was over, he returned to the Shell petroleum company and piloted his own aircraft all over the world on business for the company. For the rest of his life, Douglas Bader was an example to people who had lost limbs and he helped many of them to cope with their disabilities.

The message is ...

Many people do not allow disability to limit their activities and enjoyment of life.

Songs

One more step	*Come & Praise* 47
I can climb	*Every Colour* 17
For all the strength	*Someone's Singing, Lord* 16

A thought to share

Many disabled people got more out of life than people who are able-bodied – and they complain a great deal less.

Are you listening, God?

Father, take care of all those who have a disability and show us how we can be kind and considerate to them.

Lord, make all of us aware of the difficulties that can be encountered by people with disabilities and show us how we can make it easier for them to help themselves.

Thank you, God, for our own health and strength. Guide us so that we always make the most of these gifts that you have given us.

With Year 5 in mind

SCHOOL MATTERS

37
I know I left it there

Theme

Looking after your own property. No matter how careful parents are when marking clothing and other belongings, some children manage to 'lose' an amazing array of possessions.

Starters

1 Who has lost anything in school during the past two weeks? Why?

2 Assuming the property was not stolen by some mean person, could anything have been done to prevent the losses? By whom?

3 Some schools have 'Lost clothing parades'. Perhaps your school is one of them. If the lost property was to be laid out on the hall (class/area) floor, would you be able to identify your own property?

4 Who has lost anything at home or elsewhere during the past two weeks?

5 Did you get the blame? Was that fair?

Story

The heavenly twins

Henrietta and Harriet are twin sisters aged ten, who both lose things all the time and blame each other, and they hate each other very much. If Harriet has lost her jumper she insists that Henrietta has hidden it. If Henrietta runs around wailing that she has lost her packed lunch that Mum made just ten minutes earlier then it is always Harriet's fault.

One Saturday morning, Mrs Pobble, the next-door neighbour, asked if the twins would like to take her baby, Tarquin, for a walk. The girls were not too keen until Mrs Pobble used the magic word, 'money' and then they could not get out quickly enough. Mrs Pobble insisted that they toss a coin for who would be first to push the baby-buggy. She knew what the twins were like.

Off they went to the shopping precinct where they spent ten minutes watching a very bad juggler dropping plates and then Harriet announced that she was going to buy an iced lolly. She disappeared before Henrietta could object. Ten minutes passed and Henrietta got more and more fidgety.

Just as she was about to set off in search of her sister, Harriet returned, sucking her lolly. Henrietta started yelling at Harriet that she was selfish and Harriet called Henrietta a misery. Harriet threw the remains of the lollie at Henrietta who kicked her on the ankle, Harriet pinched her sister, Henrietta bit Harriet on the arm and they both ran home, howling.

They were running up the path to tell Mum 'how beastly my sister has been, Mum' when Mrs Pobble stopped them.

'Where's Tarquin?' she asked. The howling stopped immediately and you never saw two girls move faster than they did.

I would like to be able to tell you that the shock cured the twins. But it didn't. They are just as bad now as they have ever been. Still, they'll learn. At least, I hope so.

The message is ...

Most of us forget where we put things, now and again, but we should try not to make a habit of it.

Songs

Do your best	*Every Colour* 48
The 'Losing Things' song	*Songs for Every Day* 42
Try again	*Tinderbox* 56

A thought to share

Isn't it great when you find something you thought you'd lost?

Are you listening, God?

Thank you, God, for our possessions, however little they may be. Help us to take care of them.

Father God, teach us to value what we own and how to keep them in safe places where we can always find them.

Lord, thank you for your gifts to us. Remind us now and again that the best things in life are free.

38
Who needs a reason? *

Theme

Bullying. Most schools have a policy directed at the problem but it is good to air the subject now and again.

Starters

Avoid any personal references.

1 What is a bully?

2 Who has ever been bullied? Do you know why you were bullied?

3 Is anyone being bullied now? (You may get a response but don't hold your breath)

4 Is there ever a good reason for bullying?

5 What kind of children are bullies?

6 Why do you think they do it?

7 Has anyone here ever been a bully? Why were you a bully? Why have you stopped?

Story

A Jurassic tale

Picture a scene, millions of years ago. A blazing sun beats down on bare and craggy rocks. Clouds of yellow smoke from a towering volcano drift across a distant desert of red sand. A small creature, no more than a metre tall, scuttles across the hot stone. Its sharp teeth are snapping away at a huge flying insect, like a gigantic dragon fly, with wings as wide as your arm is long.

'Come here, insect,' yelps the dinosaur, Compsognathus, which we shall shorten to Compo, because it is easier to say. 'Keep still, can't you?'

'Not likely,' whirrs the dodging insect. 'Why should I?'

'Because,' puffs Compo, still snapping, 'I am bigger and stronger than you. And faster. So you are to be my dinner.' Snap! Large flying insect becomes the little dinosaur's dinner.

Compo trots over to a handy pool for a drink to wash down her dinner. As she bends down she feels hot breath on her scaly back. It belongs to a dinosaur, three metres tall, well-equipped with wicked teeth and nasty claws.

'Come here!' snarls Deinonychus, a most unfriendly dinosaur, which we shall call Deino for short.

'Not likely,' squeals Compo, getting ready to leave in a hurry. 'Why should I?'

'Because,' bellows Deino, 'I am bigger and stronger than you. So you are to be my dinner.' Snap, crack, munch. Compo becomes Deino's dinner.

Feeling rather full up, Deino settles down for an after-dinner nap in the shade of an over-hanging rock. She awakes, conscious that she is not alone, a very large shadow looming over her. It belongs to a dinosaur, ten metres tall, with terrifying teeth and massive claws.

'Come here!' hisses Allosaurus, the fearsome animal, to which we shall give the name Allo.

'Not likely,' roars Deino, scrambling to her feet. 'Why should I?'

'Because,' roars Allo, even more loudly, 'I am bigger and stronger than you. So you are to be my dinner.' You can imagine for yourself what happened next.

Allo is not prepared for what happens as he rests and digests his dinner.

A flock of seven flying dinosaurs, called Dimorphodon, with wings measuring two metres from tip to tip, swoops down towards the Allosaurus.

'Stand still!' screeches the biggest flier.

Allo roars, 'You must think I am stupid. Why should I?'

'Because, says the chief airborne reptile, 'we are faster and more agile than you are. You can't fly. Besides, there are seven of us. You don't stand a chance. You are to be our dinner.' And, like a swarm of screeching giant bees, the hungry flock homes in on the target ...

Footnote: Liberties have been taken with the time scale.

The message is ...

Bullies beware! There is always someone bigger and stronger than you are – to say nothing of people with more brains.

Songs

Guess how I feel	*Come & Praise* 89
Would you turn your back?	*Every Colour* 34
Don't you push me down	*Tinderbox* 26

A thought to share

Would you like someone to call you a bully?

Are you listening, God?

Lord, help us to understand that we are not being cowards if we ask for protection against bullying.

Dear God, never let us be bullies but show us how to protect those weaker than ourselves, against those who would hurt them.

Bless our school and neighbourhood, Father God, and make them happy places in which we can all feel safe.

39
Seeing and looking

Theme

Reading carefully. We often look at the printed or written word, not really absorbing what we see. Careful reading is especially important during test situations.

Starters

1 What was the last written test done by Miss X's/Mr Y's class/group/team?
2 Did you have to read the instructions? Did you understand them?
3 How many times did you have to read them before they made sense?
4 Was it easier if someone read the instructions aloud to you?
5 Who finds instructions on a computer program easy to follow? Why?
6 If things go wrong in a test or when running a program is it because you (a) misread the questions (b) could not understand them?

   If it was 6(b) why couldn't you understand them?

Story

It pays to read properly

The villainous bunch of cut-throats piled out of the boat on to the wet beach and grouped around Gruesome, the captain of the pirate ship, *Filthy*.

'Aaarrrrh!' bellowed the Cap'n, 'This be the island where old Grubby 'id the treasure. Now, the map says, 'Go north 'til us sees a big stone idol with two starin' eyes. Us has to push one eye to find out where us 'as to go next.'

First Mate Foul turned the map over and squinted at it. He said, 'Cap'n, there be summat writ on 'ere. Might be important.'

Gruesome snatched the map and scoffed, 'Us don't need to take no notice of all that. Come on, me 'earties, follow I!' He threw the map down on the sand and dashed off. Soon, they were looking up at a huge, ugly statue. Mushy, the sailmaker clambered up to the statue's head and pushed the left eye.

A huge stone spear shot out of the eye and missed skewering Mushy by the thickness of a parrot's tail. A piece of paper fluttered to the ground.

Gruesome picked it up and read, 'Wrong eye, stupid.' Squirt, the master gunner, climbed up and pushed the other eye, making sure he was not standing in front of it. The eye clanged open and Squirt read out the message inside.

'Right this time. Go one league east through the swamp and find an old hut made of black stone. Dig down six feet ten paces north from the doorway. You never know what you might find. Good luck.'

The crew trudged through the smelly, steaming swamp, dodging snakes, crocodiles and spiders, to say nothing of the lizards, and eventually found the old hut and did as the instructions said. Coxswain Gunge hopped down into the hole that they had dug and handed up a small, wooden chest to the Captain. It was quite empty. Apart from, that is, another piece of paper.

Gruesome read out, with a purple face, 'Sorry. You should have read everything on the back of the map. Love and kisses from your old seadog pal. Jeremiah Grubb.'

Everyone rushed back to the beach. When they got there, the tide had come in and gone out again. So had the map.

The message is ...

It pays to read things carefully.

Songs

Travel on	*Come & Praise* 42
Take the time to cogitate	*Every Colour* 47
Turn, turn, turn	*Alleluya* 32

A thought to share

You might save a little time if you don't read something properly but it may cost you dear later.

Are you listening, God?

Lord, give us clear minds and the ability to think.

Father, teach us to approach tasks with care and to appreciate the value of sound preparation.

Thank you, Father God, for the gift of intelligence that enables us to do our work.

40
You may never forget it

Theme

Owning up. It has been said that confession is good for the soul. Children are unlikely to be aware of such a profound truth but they often feel better if they do own up to a misdemeanour.

Starters

1 If you broke a piece of school equipment, would you own up to doing it? Why or why not?
2 If you broke, say, a toy belonging to a friend, would you own up to it? Why or why not?
3 If you broke something at home, such as a vase or a plate, would you own up to it?
4 If you did own up would you feel better for your decision?

Story

The penknife

This story is based on a true incident, many years ago.

George was really fed up with the geography lesson. He was not really interested in Tibet. To relieve the boredom, he took the new penknife out of his pocket and opened it to admire it, one blade at a time. He had been saving his pocket money for the knife for months. It was unfortunate that he should spot the two short leather straps, hanging down from beneath the desk lid in front of him.

George just had to test his penknife, to see how sharp the big blade was. Snick. Snick. The straps fell off in his sweaty palm. The blade was sharp. Then he realised what had he done and he poked the straps inside the desk. At break-time he threw the knife over a wall. He'd retrieve it later, after school.

Later, old Dobbin, the Headmaster came into the German lesson, with a face like thunder, and muttered to Frau Trotter, pointing at George as he did so. Oh, crumbs. They'd tracked him down. Somebody had seen him throw the penknife away.

'You, boy. Taylor,' barked the Head, 'Come with me,' and marched off. In his study, the Headmaster produced the severed straps and waved them under George's nose. 'You cut these off Jessica Vernon's satchel, didn't you, boy? Give me the knife.' George gritted his teeth and said, defiantly, "Never had a knife, Sir. Didn't see any straps.'

The Headmaster exploded. He yelled at him, 'You little liar, you were sitting in the girl's desk so who else could it be?'

'Not me, Sir,' George insisted, stoutly. There was no way old Dobbin was going to give him six strokes of the cane on his backside. The Headmaster produced an enormous handkerchief, mopped his forehead and shook his head, sadly. Then he looked at George with his hypnotic brown eyes, enlarged by his strong glasses.

'I give up, Taylor. I know you did it. You know you did it. God knows you did it. You are guilty. I shall not cane you because you have not admitted your guilt. Many years from now, I will have forgotten this episode. But you won't. You will remember for the rest of your life that you were too cowardly to admit you had committed a crime. Now get out of my sight.'

George felt very pleased with himself at getting away without a caning. He forgot about the incident for forty long years. Until he woke up on the morning after he had retired from work. For no particular reason, he remembered the episode of the penknife and the straps in every detail and, also for no particular reason, he suddenly felt terribly ashamed of himself.

In fact, now he is rather an old man, he remembers it quite often. I should know. That's right. I'm George.

The message is …

Owning up if you have done something is the best thing to do and you can feel proud of yourself for doing it.

Songs

You've got to move	*Come & Praise* 107
On life's highway	*Every Colour* 48
Try again	*Tinderbox* 56

A thought to share

If you do not own up when you have done something wrong or broken something by accident then someone else is sure to get the blame.

Are you listening, God?

Lord, give us the courage to admit our mistakes.

Father, forgive us for the things we have done wrong. Help us to make amends for what we have done.

Father God, may we be kind and loving in all we do.

41
Will it do?

Theme

Standards. Children (and adults) should never be satisfied with offering sub-standard work.

Starters

1 Who thinks it is important to do your best? (Everybody does, of course …)
2 Are there times when doing your best doesn't matter too much? When?

3 If you were writing, say, a composition (essay) does the handwriting/spelling/grammar matter?

4 When you are doing a maths problem, are you satisfied with an answer that is nearly correct?

5 When you are using a computer, if you input the wrong commands, what happens?

6 Are there times when it is vital that you give of your best?

Story

The royal visitor and a hut

This is a story often told by Egobo, the old storyteller of the Azamwi, a tribe that once lived on the banks of the deep, dark lake called Borondi, but is now no more.

'Many rainy seasons ago, when I was learning the art of story-telling, a messenger marched into the village of Dakwati and announced, 'The mighty King Onoko is to pass through this village tomorrow, on a long journey. He commands you to provide a new hut so that he may spend the night here.'

Ungola, chief of the village of Dakwati, sent for his eldest son.

'Yes, my father,' said Prince Kizundu, 'Do you have a task for me?'

'Yes, I do,' growled the chief. 'The king is coming here tomorrow and we have to build a hut for him. The men of the village have gone hunting and the women are in the fields. You and your lazy friends never do any work. So you can build the hut. Ashamba, master hut-builder, will tell you what to do.'

The old master gave his instructions. 'Cut long, straight branches for the frame of the hut from the Haha tree, which has *smooth* bark. Cut strong vines to lash the branches together from the Hoho tree, which has *sticky* bark.

Lastly pick the leaves to cover the frame from the Hehe tree, which has *rough* bark.'

Kizundu and his friends set off into the jungle and came to a tree with rough bark. But Kizundu had forgotten what he had been told.

'Is this a Haha tree and shall we cut its branches?' asked Kumba.

'I don't know,' laughed the Prince, 'One tree is very like another. Anyway, it will do. Cut away!'

They came to a tree with smooth bark. Kizundu still could not remember which tree was which.

'Is this a Hoho tree and shall we cut its vines?' enquired Thaka. 'I don't know,' laughed the Prince, 'One tree is very like another. Anyway, it will do. Cut away!'

They came to a tree with sticky bark. Kizundu had given up trying to remember by now.

'Is this a Hehe tree and shall we pick its leaves?' asked Elubi.

'I don't know,' giggled the Prince, 'One tree is very like another. Anyway, it will do. Pick away!' They cut and picked and built all night, until a great hut was finished.

It was not very well done, but as the four tired men looked at it with bleary eyes in the rosy light of dawn they all agreed that it would do.

The Chief got up early to inspect the work. He was not too impressed with the workmanship but there was no time to do anything about it. He, too, said, 'The King will be too tired to notice after his long journey. Oh, it will do.'

Later that day, in the blistering heat of the midday sun, the Great King arrived. The whole village celebrated his arrival with a great feast and, as night fell, the Great King went to bed in the new hut. But oh! during the night, there was a torrential storm. The lightning flashed, the thunder crashed, the rain lashed down and the wind howled.

The tropical storm was too much for the poorly-built hut. As you might expect, it fell to pieces as the branches twisted, the vines fell to shreds and the leaves all blew away. Prince Kizundu's 'It will do' had not worked out at all well. One tree was *not* like another and the materials were all wrong.

The Great King Onoko got very wet indeed and he was extremely angry. I do not know what happened next, but the last time I was in that part of the country I went to visit my cousin who lived in the village of Dakwati. But I could find no trace of her. Or anybody else. Come to that, I could not find any trace of the village. I wonder why?'

The message is ...

If you are going to do a piece of work, then 'It will do' is the best recipe for doing it badly.

Songs

Somebody greater	*Come & Praise* 5
If I had a hammer	*Every Colour* 40
Taking my time	*Songs for Every Day* 61

A thought to share

What a blessing that the great bridge-builders of the world have never said, 'It will do'.

Are you listening, God?

Lord, teach us to give of our best at all times and not to be satisfied with second-best.

Dear God, we shall have this day only once. Help us not to waste it.

Bless my hands today, Father God, and may everything I do with them be kind and helpful.

42
What a funny person

Theme

The class comedian. Most teachers have come across the juvenile clown, usually a boy. Their motives for being humorists vary from child to child but sometimes they are defensive.

Starters

Teacher: If you have your own class clown you will have to play this assembly by ear.

1 In what ways do comedians make people laugh?
2 Apart from earning a living, why do people become comedians?
3 Should we laugh at anything in a classroom?
4 Is silly behaviour by one or more children a good thing? Why?
5 What do you think about silly behaviour in a classroom?
6 Is a classroom a good place for a person who wants to make other people laugh?
7 Some children have reasons for being silly in class. What do you think those reasons might be?

Story

That's not funny

One fine summer's day, Sir Pelham of Gigglewick set out to see if there any brave deeds that he could do. You know the sort of thing I mean – rescuing maidens from tall towers and that sort of stuff. As he ambled along on his old horse, he nearly fell over a dragon in the road. He didn't like the look of this one, which had little puffs of green smoke coming from its nostrils.

'Oh, dear,' said the dragon, whose name was Doris, heaving a sigh, 'Not another stupid knight. Why can't they leave me alone?' She puffed out a few small flames and Pelham backed off, drawing his sword from its scabbard.

He waved it about a bit and said, 'I say, do you have to do that fire thingy?'

'I'm a dragon,' grunted Doris, 'And dragons scorch knights.'

'Dash it, dragon, old thing,' said Pelham, 'You aren't really going to do that, are you?' Doris sat down in the road and yawned. 'Tell you what,' she said, 'Make me laugh and I'll let you off. No frying tonight.'

Sir Pelham looked uncomfortable. 'I can't do that,' he squeaked, 'I'm not a jester. How do I make you laugh?'

'Tell me a joke,' sniggered Doris.

'I don't know any jokes,' yelped the knight, turning to run. He had only gone three paces when a blast of flame caught him on the place where he sits on his horse.

In desperation he told his joke, 'Why does a chicken cross the road?'

Little flames flickered from Doris' nostrils as she said, ominously, 'I heard that one when I was an egg, you idiot. And it wasn't funny then. Just old. You'll have to do better than that.'

Frantically, Pelham racked his brains. Then he recalled one of Jester Jingle's jokes that had amused the King.

'You'll like this,' said the knight, cheerfully, 'What does a hundred-ton dragon call the King?'

Doris growled, unpleasantly, 'And what does a hundred ton dragon call the King?'

Pelham ran towards his horse, shouting over his shoulder, 'Anything it likes!' He did not wait to find out whether Doris laughed or not but he gave up being a knight and went to Jester School to learn how to make people laugh.

I don't know how well he did, but the last time I saw him he was selling candles at the local market.

The message is ...

There is a time and a place for being funny but the classroom is not always the best theatre.

Songs

You shall go out with joy	*Come & Praise* 98
Stick on a smile	*Every Colour* 43
Maja pade – Let's all be happy	*Tinderbox* 57

A thought to share

Being able to make others laugh is a gift – if you have it don't waste it on those who have no sense of humour.

Are you listening, God?

Father, we thank you for laughter. Help us to be sure that our laughter is never cruel or mocking.

Lord, we all have different ideas of what is funny and what is not. Let us never be funny at someone else's expense.

We thank you, God, for entertainers who make us laugh but hurt no one's feelings by the things they say or do.

HOME AND AWAY

43
There are other things

Theme

Over-involvement with one activity and lack of versatility. Some children (and adults) devote all their energies to one narrow band of activity. Important they may be to the practitioner, but children should realise that their chosen activity is not their sole option.

Starters

1 Who considers themselves to be good at sport?
2 Would you like to play sport for a living?
3 In which sport? (One at a time, please ....!)
4 Why sport in preference to other jobs?
5 What are the drawbacks to being a full-time professional?
6 Who is good at other activities (such as dancing or horse-riding) and would like to do it for a living? Should those people have a 'back-up' to that sort of occupation? Why?

Story

Always have more than one string to your bow!

Note: TV 'talent' programmes as featured in this story do actually exist.

Dawn had been watching 'I'm a Star!' on TV and criticising the imitation artistes all the way through. This was her favourite programme in which brave amateur performers appear, singing live as look-alike, sound-alike copies of well-known singers, helped by wigs and clever make-up. The audience votes for the best impression of an artiste.

After the show was over, Dawn leapt up and squealed, 'I'm as good as any of them. I could imitate Whitney Houston.'

Her Mum said, 'Well, you do look rather like her. Why not give it a go?' Dawn's brother made a tape of her voice, singing to a Karaoke backing and she sent it off to the TV station.

To her astonishment, Dawn was called for an audition and was selected to appear in the third 'I'm a Star!' show on TV along with five other 'wannabes'. Dawn looked sensational – the TV programme's make-up artists and their costume department worked miracles to make her a lookalike of the real singing star. The rest was up to her. Dawn's singing certainly impressed the studio audience – the similarity of her voice to the real thing was uncanny. She could hardly believe it when the audience voted her as 'the most like' the person she was imitating. The programme's presenter, Ben O'Reilly, said that the resemblance was quite amazing. Even then, Dawn did not really think she would get beyond this first round.

But she did. She appeared in the final show, along with seven other performers, imitating stars from modern show business and earlier years – Cliff Richard, Jarvis Cocker and all.

Can you imagine Dawn's intense excitement when she was voted the winner, but this time by a telephone vote from viewers and not just the studio audience. Her prize was £1000 and the promise of a record contract and Dawn thought no more about it after the excitement of winning had subsided.

She was not prepared for the phone call asking her to go to the famous Church Street recording studios in London but she felt as if her dreams were coming true.

There, guided by the record producer, Art Zolto, she performed a demo disc of 'Never leave me' the song she had sung in the competition.

Joe Tyreman, the record company's publicity manager listened to the session. He was very pleased and said, 'How about you doing another number?' There was an embarrassed silence. 'I can't do any other songs,' said Dawn, sheepishly.

Joe's cigar fell out of his mouth and he said, as if he did not believe it, 'Oh come on. Go away and practise. Come back this time next week and show me what you can do. You can't just perform one song and become a *star*?'

Dawn did. She practised and practised and she was ... terrible. Joe nearly cried when he heard the new song.

'Honey,' he whimpered, 'You need more than one string to your bow if you are going to make it in show business. Just forget the whole idea, huh?' And with that he walked out of the studio.

A lot of tears flowed from the budding star but the record producer was right – one song does not make a star – and Dawn knew it.

So did her Mum.

That was the end of Dawn's singing career. She decided to train as a hairdresser and to be *herself* because she knew there were many other things that she could do without imitating anyone else and, what is more, do them well.

The message is ...

Nobody should concentrate on doing just one thing well, especially if it requires top physical fitness or the use of the voice, because there may come a time you need to do something else for a living.

Songs

The journey of life	*Come & Praise* 45
I can climb	*Every Colour* 17
Football crazy	*Jolly Herring* 15

A thought to share

What do professional sportsmen and dancers do when they retire?

Are you listening, God?

Thank you, Father for our talents, whatever they may be. Help us not to waste them.

Lord, give us the wisdom to realise that we should do our best to excel at more than one thing. Make us wise enough to do our best whatever we may try.

Give us, Father God, helping hands and a loving heart in whatever we do.

44
You might think it's Art

Theme

Graffiti. The practice of adorning walls, etc, with graffiti is anti-social, anti-environment and, taken to extreme lengths, a criminal activity. Some people do it full-time …

Starters

1 Who knows what we call words and pictures that are sprayed on to walls and other places?
2 Who likes looking at it? Why? Or why not?
3 Who would like to do it? Why?
4 Does it improve blank walls etc? Or the opposite?
5 For whose benefit is it done?
6 Do you think people should be sent to prison for doing it? Or should there be some other punishment? Should there be any punishment at all?
7 Would this school be any the better for having pictures and slogans sprayed on to the walls?

Story

This is based on a true newspaper report.

What an artist!

'It was pretty unfair, I reckon,' whined Sidney, 'I got five years in the nick for decorating some boring walls. And buses. And trains and cars. And bridges and buildings. And a London tube train. Once.'

Elmer whistled, 'That's a bit stiff.'

'Yeah,' moaned Sidney, 'Stupid old judge said I was a vandal. Me! A vandal. I tell you, pal, I'm an artist. OK, so I use a spray-can instead of a brush.'

'But such a long stretch for spraying a few little pictures?' asked Elmer.

'Listen, pal,' boasted Sidney, 'All my pictures were big, man, big! That's why the Old Bill took away over 400 spray-cans from my bedroom and all sorts of things I needed for my art work like a map of places that I had brightened up.'

Elmer's face lit up. Then he said, brightly, 'I read about you in the paper last week? Called yourself Bisto or something, didn't you?' Sidney corrected him, 'Not 'Bisto', you twit. Tosto. All the graffiti gangs – the crews – reckoned I was one of the best, if not the best.'

Elmer scratched his spiky head and said, 'Well, I reckon it was all a waste of paint. What a waste of talent. What a lot of porridge. Do you go to art classes in here?' Sidney nodded.

His cell-mate shook his head, 'Should have done that before, you nutter. Then you might have made a living out of it. Instead of making a mess of all those walls. Still, I'm only an old burglar. What do I know?'

The message is ...

Graffiti is one of the worst forms of vandalism and nobody appreciates graffiti except the people who put it there.

Songs

For the beauty of the earth	Come & Praise 11
Look around	Every Colour 9
Sing a song of people	Tinderbox 18

A thought to share

What would graffiti vandals do if aerosols were banned?

Are you listening, God?

Lord, teach us how to look after the places where we live.

Father God, help us to realise that what is beautiful to one person may well be ugly to another.

God, our Father, give us the wisdom to understand that nobody else wants to read what we write on walls.

45
So it was liberated?

Theme

Euphemisms for the word 'stealing'. Less criminality seems to be attached to words such as 'nicking,' 'shop-lifting', 'half-inching' (rhyming slang for 'pinching') than it does for the blunt use of 'stealing'.

Starters

1 Is it honest to nick things belonging to someone else?

2 Is it honest to lift things belonging to someone else?

3 Is it honest to pinch things from someone else?

4 Is it honest to purloin things from someone else? (Children might not know what 'purloin' means but it is not slang, anyway.)

5 What's the difference between nicking, lifting, pinching, purloining and stealing?

Story

The blue vase

What happened to the vase (a real blue Meissen vase, c.1922) is true although the characters are fictitious.

Seven-year old Jayne looked up from the magazine she was reading. 'Grandad,' she said, quizzically, 'What's 'liberating' mean?'

Tom Grant put down his newspaper and enquired, 'Where on earth did you find words like that, pet?'

'In this magazine of Grannie's,' she said. 'It says, 'The castle was liberated by the King's soldiers that same afternoon.'

'Oh, I see,' said Tom, 'Well, it means that people have been set free from whoever captured them. Like we liberated the French people from the Nazis in the Second World War. I helped, because I was in the Army.'

'I know,' Jayne said, peevishly, 'You've told me that a hundred times.

Nearly as many times as you've showed me your medals.' Tom pretended not to hear and turned back to the football page. But not for long.

'Grandad,' said Jayne, sitting up. Tom groaned and took his glasses off again.

'If 'liberating' means setting people free, why do you say you 'liberated' that blue vase on the top shelf of the china cabinet? Did you set it free?' Tom had a feeling he was letting himself in for a difficult few minutes.

He said, uncomfortably, 'Well, er, no, not exactly. It was standing all alone on a shelf in a big German castle. So I, er, liberated it, put it in the tank I was driving and brought it home with me after the war was over.'

Looking very thoughtful, Jayne said, 'Who did it belong to?'

'I don't know!' said Tom, becoming irritated. He had never thought about it. He knew what was coming next.

'So nobody said you could have it?' said his grand-daughter, standing up, looking very angry, 'You stole it, didn't you? I'm ashamed of you, Grandad.'

'Oh, come on, love, it was more than fifty years ago,' protested Tom, 'and everybody was liberating things.'

'Humph,' announced his grand-daughter, folding her arms. 'It doesn't matter how long ago it was. And that sort of liberating means stealing, so there. I never thought my Grandad was a stealer. I'm going to tell Grannie.' She stormed out of the room leaving her grandfather with a lot to think about.

The message is …

Stealing is stealing, whatever other name may be used for the act or whatever the circumstances under which it is done.

Songs

It's a new day	*Come & Praise* 106
Song of life	*Every Colour* 22
Turn, turn, turn	*Alleluya* 32

A thought to share

If you take another person's belongings without telling them have you committed a crime?

Are you listening, God?

Father God, we know the difference between right and wrong. Let us never be afraid to do what is right but make us ashamed when we do wrong.

Lord, teach us to respect other people's property, just as we expect them to respect ours.

Remind us, Father, from time to time, that being honest is something of which we can be proud.

46
Look after them

Theme

Caring for pets. Everyone who has pets should care for them, but some people seem to take their concern rather a long way.

Starters

1 Who has pets at home?
2 Who looks after them?
3 In what way are they looked after?
4 Do you think that pets are as important as human beings? Why?
5 What do you think of people who leave a lot of money, when they die, to their pets?
6 If you think it is wrong, to whom should the money be left if there are no relatives to inherit the money?
7 Is it anybody else's business?

Story

This story is based on a true newspaper report.
If cats could *talk* …

A Land of milk and money

'Time to go home, Sprat,' said Fluff sadly, looking up at the full moon, 'Things will never be the same again, will they?'

Sprat shook his head and said, 'No more sitting on the garden wall and talking about the good old days when we were kittens?' Suddenly he burst into catty tears and sobbed and sobbed. 'It's not my fault, Spratty,' Fluff said, apologetically, 'I didn't ask to be left thirty thousand pounds.' Sprat wiped his nose and said, 'Why did your mistress, old Flo Mooney, do it?'

Fluff shook his head and said, 'I have no idea. I know she used to make me sick with her drooling over me and telling me what a beautiful pussy I am. But thirty thousand …'

'It's not the first time a pet has been left a fortune,' mewed Sprat. 'Do you remember that awful, pampered poodle that lived in High Close House? It was called Diddly Doo or something equally horrible.'

Fluff snarled as only a cat can, 'Huh. You mean the one that ate nothing but minced chicken and thin slices of toast and its mistress used to clean its teeth after every meal. With its own gold-plated toothbrush and fluoride toothpaste.' Sprat began to cat-laugh helplessly and fell off the wall. Shaking off the soil that had stuck to his fur he jumped back on to the wall, where he began to clean himself with his rough tongue.

'What is going to happen to all that money?' Sprat asked, '*You* can't spend it. You're only a *cat*.'

Fluff heaved a sigh. 'I heard Flo's niece saying that I was being sent to live at the Choosy home for retired cats, in Grassdown. Pampered pussies there live on a diet of fresh fish and rich milk. I shall probably become a fat cat and die from being overweight,' he said, trying to sound casual about it.

'But you could never eat your way through thirty thousand pounds worth of fish!' yowled Sprat and burst out cat-laughing. Fluff joined him and their cats' chorus could be heard streets away. Then Fluff became quite serious and he mewed thoughtfully, 'I would have thought that my Miss Mooney's money could have been used to help animals that have had a rough life – you know, like donkeys or monkeys or animals that have been cruelly treated.' 'That's right' said Sprat, thoughtfully, 'There's a place in Devon for donkeys and one in Dorset for monkeys, I believe.'

'Yes,' purred Fluff, 'and even a place where poorly and injured hedgehogs are cared for. I think it's called Mrs Tiggywinkle's, you know, after the hedgehog in the Beatrix Potter story. Now *they* can always do with some money. Not that I'm too keen on hedgehogs. Those prickles play havoc with my nose, you know, even if you are only trying to be friendly.'

'And,' said Sprat, nodding his agreement, 'most important of all, there are places where sick and injured *cats* are cared for. I think something called the Cat Protection League runs them.'

Fluff looked a little uncomfortable, and said hesitantly, 'Er … and … er … there are places for … D-O-G-S, too.' 'Humph,' cat-snorted Sprat, 'The less said about *them* the better. I don't get on with *them*.'

Fluff cleaned his whiskers to cover his embarrassment and went on, 'Still, not much *we* can do about giving any of them money, is there my old pal?'

'Nothing at all,' agreed Sprat, shaking his head. 'After all, we are only cats. And nobody ever asks us *our* opinion.'

The message is …

Look after your pets, but you don't have to spend a lot of money on them to show that you care about them.

Songs

All the animals	*Come & Praise* 80
Take care of a friend	*Every Colour* 35
All things that live	*Someone's Singing, Lord* 41

A thought to share

Would your pet still be loyal to you if you did not feed it?

Are you listening, God?

Lord, take care of all our pets and help us to care for them in the proper way, being kind to them at all times.

Father, make us wise towards our pets and remind us now and again that they are not human beings, however much we may love them.

Thank you, God, for our pets and for the pleasure they give us. Let us never tease them nor treat them with cruelty.

47
Something for nothing

Theme

Pocket money. Children receive varying amounts of pocket money although it may have other names.

Starters

1 Who gets pocket money?
2 Who doesn't ? (You won't get many takers ...)
3 What kind of amounts? (Expect some extravagant claims ...)
4 Who has to do jobs for their pocket money?
5 What sort of jobs?
6 Who thinks they should not have to do jobs in exchange for pocket money? Why not?

Story

Money for nothing

Each month, a wealthy merchant summoned his four eldest sons to his shop and gave them each five gold coins. The fifth and youngest son, Amyas, received nothing. Although his four elder brothers never seemed to seek work, Amyas never complained, even though he worked hard in his father's shop. One day, his father asked him whether he felt badly treated because he received no wages whereas his idle brothers did.

'I do not mind working for you for no reward. Are you not my father?' said Amyas, cheerfully.

The merchant smiled fondly at his son and told him, 'Be patient yet a little while and you shall receive your due reward. So shall your brothers.' No more was said until Amyas reached the day when he was eighteen.

On that day, the Merchant called all the family into his shop and announced, 'I have decided to retire from trading and to hand over the shop as an inheritance.' There was a great hubbub as the four eldest sons argued as to who should have what and how the profits from the shop should be divided.

The merchant clapped his hands roared, 'Silence! My four eldest are entitled to nothing. For years, you have taken money from me and never suggested that you might do a service for me in return.'

'We are your sons,' shouted Abel, angrily, 'We are entitled to an allowance and our inheritance!'

Their father said, 'No child should receive money from parents and do nothing in return, if they are able. And you are no exception.' With that, he gave the key of the shop to his youngest son. What is more, Amyas did not have to ask why.

The message is …

Those who are able to work for their wages should do so unless they are sick or there is no work for them to do.

Songs

We are climbing	*Come & Praise* 49
On a work day I work	*Every Colour* 24
Work calypso	*Tinderbox* 23

A thought to share

Would you like it if you had to pay your parents for your food?

Are you listening, God?

Father God, thank you for our homes and for those who love and care for us.

Lord, help us to realise that giving a helping hand at home might be appreciated.

Show us, dear God, how we can be kind and helpful at home and how we can share the chores as well as the pleasures.

48
RAMS, ROMS and other animals

Theme

Computeritis. Obsession with computers is something of which we should all be aware and guard against.

Starters

1 Who likes using a computer?
2 Who does not?
3 What are the dangers of spending many hours operating a computer? (not possible medical implications)
4 Who thinks that it does not matter how much time you spend?

Poem

The Alarming tale of Tom, who was a Computer Buff

A bright young lad by name of Tom
Spent all his days entranced by ROM
And RAM and floppies, bytes and bits;
The boy did little else but sit
Transfixed by his computer screen,
No matter what the outside scene;
Rain, hail or snow was all the same
What mattered was computer games.
Tom did not move, nor hardly eat,
He seemed to be stuck to his seat
And after sitting for three weeks,
His clothes (and he) began to reek.
His mother told him he was dirty,

But Tommy snapped 'Oh, Qwerty, Qwerty!
(Which on a keyboard you will see
With great familiarity).
He almost lost the power of speech
And found it difficult to reach
To push a disk into the tower,
His muscles seemed to lose their power.
By now, his odour filled the house
He started talking to his 'mouse'.
For weeks computer games Tom played,
His father now was quite afraid,
Convinced obsession had set in,
Said, 'Put the keyboard in the bin!'
But Tom worked out a way to get
Connected to the Internet.
And so another week went by.
His mother uttered many sighs,
Because her son was skin and bone;
All she could do was wail and groan.
His granny said, 'Your son's at risk,'
Tom said no more than, 'Pass that disk.'
He tried to feed it in the slot,
Hard as he tried, he just could not.
So then they dragged him off his chair
Or else he'd still be sitting there;
His father said, 'Are we too late?'
The surgeon said, 'I can update.
Install a chip within his brain
And make him functional again.'
The operation took two days,
Now Tom can only say, 'Erase',
'Virus', 'Tablet' and 'Spreadsheet'
And these four words the boy repeats.
So find some other things to do
'Computeritis' could strike ... you!

The message is ...

Computers are wonderful – but they can take over!

Songs

You've got to move	*Come & Praise* 107
My mind to me a kingdom is	*Every Colour* 18
The world is big	*Tinderbox* 33

A thought to share

Can anybody make a friend of a mouse?

Are you listening, God?

Dear God, thank you for computers and the marvels they can perform but let us never exchange them for our friends.

Father of us all, give us the good sense not to spend all our time with computers but to realise that the world is full of other wonderful things.

We thank you, Lord, for technology and the wonders of science but let us not ignore the beauty in our lives.

━━━━━━ THAT'S LIFE! ━━━━━━

49
Smash and be happy!

Theme

Vandalism. Vandalism is easy to define – it is the wanton and meaningless destruction of the whole environment. Key Stage 2 children are less prone to vandalism than older practitioners, most of whom are probably still at school.

Starters

1 What do we call people who break things for fun?

2 Where does the word 'vandal' come from?
(*Teacher*: You probably already know but, to refresh your memory, the word is derived from the name of a Germanic tribe that ravaged Europe in the 4th and 5th centuries, destroying books and works of art.)

3 Why do you think children sometimes become vandals, especially when they grow into teenagers? (Don't they …?)

4 Can you suggest any ways of controlling vandals?

Story

Humbert gets upset

Long ago, in the German village of Knockenburg, there lived a very friendly giant by the name of Humbert. He did his best to get on with everyone despite being 45 metres tall and weighing 1000 kilogrammes.

The villagers built him a house and sent him food and drink. He earned his keep by doing useful chores like pulling up trees or pulling along six ploughs all at once. And, so long as he kept out of the village, there was no problem.

One day, he heard that the Burgermeister's daughter was getting married. Humbert had never seen a wedding and wanted to find out what it was like. He turned up at the edge of the village and enjoyed it all very much without getting in anyone's way. All went well until Humbert had a bout of hiccups. The horses drawing the bridal carriage bolted, flinging the bride and groom out and into the mud. The bride's mother was so startled that she had hysterics, and the priest fainted.

Humbert leaned over the church steeple to pick up the bride and groom and the steeple buckled and bent, flinging the weathercock, which narrowly missed the Mayor, on to the ground.. The Mayor lost his temper and called Humbert a big booby, a massive moron and, worst of all – a mammoth vandal! Now Humbert was not a very bright giant but he knew what that meant.

He picked up the Mayor and held the terrified man close up to his mighty nose, growling at him, 'I am not a vandal, Mister Mayor, I am not. Vandals are folk that break and smash and destroy things because they enjoy doing it. I don't mean to do it and I don't like doing it. So don't ever call me a vandal. Or I might lose my temper.' He put the trembling Mayor back on the ground more gently than he deserved and walked away.

Nobody ever saw Humbert again and nobody knew where he went. But everybody agreed that what the Mayor had said about the giant was quite wrong. He was no vandal – just big.

The message is ...

People who enjoy wrecking things such as property and trees are to be despised.

Songs

Think of a world without any flowers	*Come & Praise* 17
The world is such a lovely place	*Every Colour* 8
The angry song	*Tinderbox* 9

A thought to share

What will the vandals do when there is nothing left to smash?

Are you listening, God?

Thank you, Lord, for our lovely world. Let us never do anything to spoil it.

Father, bring wisdom and sense to those whom we call vandals.

Dear God, show us how we can play our part in caring for our neighbourhood and all things in it that are provided for our benefit.

50
Bigger and better

Theme

Exaggeration. Some children have a curious habit of claiming that they live in a bigger house, ride in a bigger car and go on more exotic holidays and so on, than they really do. They do not practise being mini-Munchausens to escape punishment or for personal gain; they just seek to impress – but they are telling lies and boasting, often without real cause, all the same.

Starters

1 Why do some children always claim to have to have something bigger, better and more expensive than others?
2 Who knows someone who is always boasting? (No names)
3 Do they boast about something real? Or is it in their imagination?
4 Do such children usually get found out – if their claims are not real?
5 Are children who boast, even if they have a reason to do so, popular?
6 Is any kind of boasting a good thing?

Story

Tall stories and very tall stories

'Hello there, me old hearty,' said Walter, shaking Horatio's hand, enthusiastically. I ain't seen you since …'

'Since we met in Porthampton, me boy,' interrupted Horatio, 'Just after I come back from sailin' with old Rustybeard, the worst pirate what ever roamed the Caribbean. When I were telling ee about that there sea-serpent us saw off Trinidad.'

Walter looked uncertain, then said, 'Was that the one as you reckoned was fifty feet long?'

Horatio said, shaking his head, 'Oh, no, you must have forgot. 'Twere an 'undred feet at least. Never seen the likes of it.'

Walter nodded and said, 'Don't suppose you have, Horatio. And what about that whale you said you saw off Saint Kitts? Three 'undred feet long and weighing nigh on two hundred tons, weren't it?'

Horatio went on, 'Oh ar. An' I never did tell ee, Walter, did I, about that there octopus I come across when I went overboard off Saint Vincent in '88? Tentacles two 'undred foot long it 'ad. Come at our old ship it did and grabbed a whole dinghy what us had in tow, oars and all. Never saw it again.'

Walter said, an amused expression on his face, 'Quite amazing, Horatio, the things you've seen. What a life you've had. I wish …'

He was interrupted by the landlord who growled, 'I do wish you would stop telling your tall stories, Horatio. You ain't never been on anything bigger than the old ferry boat that you rowed across the Dribble river in Porthampton for thirty years.'

Walter burst out laughing. 'Give him another rum, landlord,' he chortled, 'I knows they are tall stories. Still, no harm done. I enjoy them. But not half as much as Horatio does, I suspect!'

Horatio drank his rum and joined in with the laughter because he knew that, although his stories were extremely tall, nobody believed them. Least of all, himself.

The message is …

Those who claim to have possessions, or to have done things, on a bigger scale than is real are often people who are have difficulty in making real friends. It is best to ignore the stories and find out what the story-teller *really* wants.

Songs

Simple gifts	*Come & Praise* 97
Do your best	*Every Colour* 48
All alone in my quiet head	*Tinderbox* 17

A thought to share

If you claim you have 'been there, done that, got the Tee-shirt' and you haven't, have you ever stopped to ask yourself why you are making such claims?

Are you listening, God?

Father, help us to distinguish between truth and falsehood.

Lord, if we must boast, let us have good reasons to do so.

Father God, teach us not to make false claims about things we do not have and places we have never visited.

51
The best policy

Theme

Honesty. Most children are basically honest and this should be recognised as well as pointing out that honesty is a desirable personal quality.

Starters

1 If you saw someone drop a ten-pound note on the floor and they were not aware of it, what would you do? (100% honesty?)

2 If you saw a ten-pound note on the floor and there was no way of knowing who it belonged to, what would you do? Why?

3 If you saw that someone had left a watch in the changing-rooms (or whatever your facilities are), what would you do? (100% honesty?)

4 If you saw a bag of crisps left in the dining-area (or whatever your facilities are) and no one seemed to want them, what would you do?

Story

The traveller

A tinker, whose name was Boyd, was going to market to sell his pots and pans, made of good iron and copper. They were loaded in a large willow basket on the back of his donkey. To his dismay, the donkey stumbled and the basket fell off her back, bursting open. And, before

Boyd could stop them, the pots and pans rolled down a rabbit hole.

As Boyd looked down the hole, an ugly little man, wearing a green hat, strolled out in front of him.

The troll, for so it was, chuckled and said in a thin, reedy voice, 'Why, Boyd o'Tamdillie, what have you lost?'

Boyd answered boldly, 'All my pots and pans have rolled down that rabbit hole.'

'Be calm, my lad,' carolled the troll, 'Just dip your hand down that hole.' Boyd did so and pulled out pot after pan. To his astonishment, they were made of shining silver.

'These are not mine!' cried Boyd, 'and I want no part of them for they do not belong to me.'

'Then return them to the rabbits!' carolled the troll. Boyd did as he was bid.

'Now try again,' chuckled the troll. Boyd did as he was bid and pulled out pan after pot made of glistening gold.

'These are not mine!' cried Boyd, 'and I want no part of them for they do not belong to me.'

'Then return them to the rabbits!' laughed the troll. Boyd did as he was bid.

To his surprise, the troll laughed so much that he rolled around in the dust until he was grey all over.

'Bless my bimbamboomery, Boyd boy!' he laughed. 'You must be the most honest man I ever met. I tell you true, one like you must have his just reward. Look in your willow basket and you shall find it. And what is in there is yours and let no man say it is not.' With that, there was a bang and a flash and the troll disappeared in a puff of red smoke.

Nervously, Boyd peeked inside his willow basket which lay in the heather on the side of the road. It was full to the brim with gold coins.

Now Boyd felt happier. The coins were in his basket and no one could say other than that they had been given to him.

And you can choose to believe that or not, as you please. It makes no difference to me. I am too honest to say otherwise.

The message is ...

You never know what is going to happen when you are completely honest, but it is more likely to be something good.

Songs

A still, small voice	*Come & Praise* 96
Seeds of kindness	*Every Colour* 42
Both sides now	*Alleluya* 33

A thought to share

It is a great feeling to be trusted by everyone because they know you are honest.

Are you listening, God?

Help us, dear Lord, to be honest and trustworthy in all that we do.

Father God, remind us that being honest is right and being dishonest is wrong.

Teach us, good Lord, that there is more merit in taking the right and honest path than in following any other.

52
Someone has to win

Theme

Winning and losing. All children like to win, whether it is in sport or in other activities. Some schools do not encourage the concept of competition but there comes a time when children have to face its realities. Competition can be healthy provided children understand that it is not the only thing that matters.

Starters

1 Who likes to win, in whatever kind of competition they are taking part?

2 Who thinks winning is less important than taking part?

3 If you think it is the only reason for taking part in a contest of some sort, can you say why?

4 Who would take part in a contest if you had no hope of winning?

5 Would you take part if there was no prize?

Story

Anything you can do I can do better

Three young monkeys never stopped talking. They chattered incessantly all day – up in the trees, down on the ground, picking fruit and drinking in the river, they never stopped.

One steaming jungle morning, they were gabbling so much as they got ready for berry-picking, that their mother could stand it no longer.

'For gorilla's sake, can't you be quiet for five minutes?' she screeched, 'You never stop talking. What is more, I don't think you can stop talking.' The three young monkeys looked quite hurt.

'Well, I can stop any time I want to,' announced the eldest monkey.

'I know I can,' boasted the next eldest monkey.

'And I am *positive* that I could stop talking as soon as I make up my mind to do so,' crowed the youngest monkey. Their mother shook her head and smiled a secret smile.

'I don't believe you could,' she laughed. The three children bounced up and down in anger, as monkeys do.

'Oh, yes, we can,' they screamed angrily in unison.

'All right,' said Mother Monkey, still smiling, 'Let's make a competition out of it. The one who stays silent the longest shall have a prize.' But she steadfastly refused to tell them what the prize would be.

True to their resolutions, the monkeys did not speak to one another, or to any monkey for that matter, all the morning as they hunted for jimjam tree berries, which, as everyone knows, are quite delicious to eat.

As they were picking on a low branch a cunning old leopard came loping along, silently and sleekly as leopards do, looking for *his* breakfast. Now, as you know, leopards do not eat jimjam tree berries or any other berries for that matter because they are not vegetarians. So, when he saw the three little monkeys, he started to lick his spotty chops.

The eldest monkey saw the leopard, but he was so determined to win the competition and the prize that he kept absolutely quiet and uttered not a word of warning.

The next eldest monkey saw the leopard, too, but he was just as

determined as his brother that *he* was going to win the competition and
the prize. So he kept absolutely quiet and uttered not a word of
warning.

The youngest monkey did not even see the leopard and I shall not
tell you what happened to him because it is too awful to relate.

On the way home, the two remaining monkey brothers felt thirsty.
They had both eaten a lot of berries. So they stopped off at the river
for a drink of the cool water.

As they drank, along came a crafty old crocodile who was looking for
her breakfast. Now, as you know, crocodiles are not vegetarians either,
and when this crocodile saw the two monkeys, she started to gnash her
ferocious teeth.

The eldest monkey saw the crocodile but he was so determined to
win the competition and the prize that he kept absolutely quiet and
uttered not a word of warning.

The next eldest monkey did not even see the crocodile and I would
not care to shock you by telling you what happened to him, because
his fate was too dreadful to relate.

By this time, the eldest monkey realised how stupid he had been.
There was nothing wrong with the competition but he had not been
at all sensible in the way he had stuck to the rules. He was too ashamed
to go home so he ran away, not knowing where he was going.

And, so far as I know, he is still wherever he ran to. Wherever that
may be.

The message is ...

It is good to win but not at any cost.

Songs

Travel on	*Come & Praise* 42
Working together	*Every Colour* 37
Try again	*Tinderbox* 57

A thought to share

Remember, in a race, there are more losers than winners.

Are you listening, God?

Thank you, Father, for the chance to take part in sport. Help us to do
our best and to put playing fair above winning.

Lord, teach us not to be winners at all costs.

Father God, make us modest when we win and generous when we lose. Make us fair winners and good losers.

53
Does the world revolve around you?

Theme

Over-estimating one's importance. Nobody is indispensable. Ask any retired headteacher …

Starters

1 Who is the most important person in the country? Why?
2 Who is the most important person in this school? Why?
3 If the headteacher left the school tomorrow would the school still go on without her/him? How?
4 Who is the most important person in your home? Why?
5 Who is the most important person in the world? Why?

Story

What a performance!

'Absolutely fabulous, Odette, I have never seen a better performance,' trilled Miss Desmond, 'However, the rest of you will just have to concentrate much harder on the big night. This has been a dreadful dress rehearsal and if it were not for Odette the whole thing would have been a complete washout.'

Odette looked around smugly at the rest of the cast of 'The Secret Dance', telling herself that the teacher was dead right, she was by far the best actor in the whole school.

'Dizzy Dezzy's right, you know,' she said, haughtily, in the dressing room, 'Some of you will have to take it a bit more seriously if our parents are going to see a good show. If it wasn't for me, there wouldn't be a show at all.' She dodged the shower of scripts that were thrown at her as she made her hurried exit from the school hall.

That night, as Odette was settling down to sleep, her Dad put his head round the door and said, 'Can't make the show tomorrow, darling. I've got a late meeting at the office. Still, break a leg, eh? Isn't that what actors say because saying 'Good luck' is bad luck? Sleep tight.' Little did he know what a prophet he was ...

Next morning, Odette's Mum leapt out of bed as she heard screaming coming from the bathroom. Through the steam she could see Odette lying in the shower, holding her leg. Two hours later, Odette was in hospital having her broken leg set. She was not in much pain but she was kicking up a terrible fuss and none of the nurses could pacify her. She howled and bawled and wailed that the show could not go on that night and it would have to be cancelled because she was the star of the show and no one else could do the dances like her and no one else knew the lines and Daphne Trump was useless as an understudy and the whole thing would be a flop. Then she went to sleep.

On Saturday morning, her mother told her that the show had gone on, it had been a great success and Daphne Trump had done extremely well under the circumstances. Naturally, Odette sulked for a few days but, by the time she was home again and walking on her plaster cast, she had to admit that it is surprising how others can manage without the person who thinks they are of vital importance.

Or, if you like long words, nobody is indispensable.

The message is ...

No matter how important and essential you think you are, it is surprising that people can manage without you if they have to.

Songs

A living song	*Come & Praise* 72
Working together	*Every Colour* 37
Love somebody	*Tinderbox* 16

A thought to share

Are you really the most important person in your world?

Are you listening, God?

Lord, help us to realise that not everyone thinks we are wonderful, even if we do.

Father God, give us the sense to know that, even if we are good at something, we impress no one if we boast about it.

Teach us, dear God, that the finest achievements are made by those who are the most modest.

54
Good vibrations*

Theme

Overcoming hearing impairment – the achievements of Evelyn Glennie. The narrative gives a short account of the life and career of the well-known percussionist, who is profoundly deaf.

Starters

The 'Starters' are more by way of a general consideration of the problems of hearing impairment. This term may have to be explained to some children.

1 Who knows anyone who cannot hear very well or not at all?
2 Is that person old or young?
3 Who knows how hearing-impaired people communicate with others? (Various sign languages (signing) and lip-reading)
4 How do the TV channels help people who are hearing-impaired?
5 How can we make life less difficult for people who are hearing-impaired?

Narrative

Feel the sound!

Try watching a TV pop show or a musical concert with the sound turned off. Can you appreciate it? Difficult, isn't it? Now, can you imagine anyone appreciating music when they cannot hear it? Even more unlikely, can you imagine someone being able to tell you exactly what music is being played and then playing it for you?

Stretch your imagination even further and picture someone who cannot hear at all, not only playing percussion instruments like xylophones and drums – but playing them as a soloist with great symphony orchestras, in front of big audiences. Not only that, but imagine being hailed as one of the greatest percussionists ever.

What about composing music and recording it on tape and CD but not being able to hear any of it – at least, not as hearing people can. It takes some imagination, doesn't it?

If you go to a rave or a disco it is possible to feel the vibrations from a high-powered bass beat. The percussionist, whose name is Evelyn Glennie, does exactly that; but she has developed it to such a degree that she can tell what instrument is being played and at what pitch. She can play hundreds of different kinds of percussion instruments, including the piano.

Evelyn was very musical as child and learnt the piano, recorder and clarinet at an early age. When she began, gradually, to lose her hearing at the age of eight, no one ever expected her to become a superb percussionist who would tour the world performing with the world's great orchestras, write music, appear on TV and record music.

She was born in 1965, needed a hearing-aid by the time she was eleven and, by the time she was sixteen she could hardly hear at all. Even then, she was able to play such instruments as the piano, xylophone, glockenspiel, tympani and drums well enough to perform to a very high standard in public. At seventeen, Evelyn went to the Royal Academy of Music, won many prizes and and gained a degree. In 1989, she gave her first major public performance as a solo percussionist.

How does she do it? She has what is known as 'perfect pitch', which means she can hear the precise pitch of a note in her head and place it in relation to other notes. She says she does not need to listen to music because she can read it exactly like a book. Besides this, Evelyn knows exactly what sound occurs if she plays or strikes an instrument. She actually feels the sound through her feet, lower body and her hands, different pitch affecting her hands, arms and upper body in different ways. She can also identify notes on a drum by the tightness or slackness of the drumskin and the way the drumstick bounces off it.

So, everyone who says they can't do it, whatever it is, should think of people like Evelyn Glennie, who can't hear a thing, and yet has gone on to become one of the world's finest musicians. Then you might be surprised what you can do.

The message is ...

It is amazing how some people can overcome huge obstacles and become the best – all because of determination and courage.

Songs

If I had a hammer	*Come & Praise* 71
	(and *Every Colour* 40)
Can you hear?	*Harlequin* 33
Sound waves	*Flying a Round* 59

A thought to share

Most people have great sympathy with people who cannot see but are we considerate enough with those who cannot hear?

Are you listening, God?

We thank you, dear Lord, for the sense of hearing. Teach us to be generous to those who do not have this gift in full or not at all.

Father God, we are grateful for the gift of music and for the means of making music. Help us to consider other people when we are enjoying our own kind of music so that it does not offend them.

God of us all, show us how to appreciate and understand all music and give us the determination we need to master the making of music, whether by voice or by instrument.

With Year 6 in mind
━━ SCHOOL MATTERS ━━

55
A little forethought

Theme

The advantages of planning properly. Planning a piece of work usually results in a better end-product.

Starters

1 What should you think of if you are planning to write a story?
2 If you are planning to write a play, do you have to think of something more than if you are writing a story?
3 Can anyone suggest some other situations in which it is advisable to plan ahead?
4 Can one over-plan?

Story

On solid ground

Long ago, a mighty king decided he wanted a palace built where he could calm his nerves by watching the sea. Three architects prepared plans, and were told to build their version of the new palace on any site that they decided was the most suitable – at their own expense! The architect of the design that pleased the king most would receive ten thousand gold pieces and another five thousand to the architect whose design was completed first. The others would receive nothing.

The first architect, Amata, chose the first site he saw, on the edge of the cliff known as the Golden Drop. The second architect, Basilio, also chose the first site that he saw on the edge of the cliff known as the Yellow Height. The third architect, Constanti, searched all along the coast for a suitable site. Eventually, he chose one known as the Red

Sheer and set his men to work, but they were many weeks behind those of his rivals.

A year passed and the king decided to find out for himself how the building was proceeding. When he reached Amata's site there was nothing to be seen. The whole palace had slipped into the sea even before it was finished.

'The fool has built on soft sandstone!' cried the king. 'He should have found this out before building began.' He arrived at Basilio's palace just in time to see it too slide into the boiling sea below.

'The fool has built on loose shale!' cried the king. 'He should have found this out before building began.' He arrived at Constanti's palace, but was surprised to see that it was unfinished.

Before the king could say a word, Constanti said, 'Great Majesty, before you criticise me, please bear in mind that I spent many weeks looking for solid ground for the palace. And, when I found it, building was more difficult because the rock was so hard for sinking the foundations. But no storm can wash away this cliff, because it is made from ironstone and granite.' The king was satisfied with this explanation and was content to wait until the palace was built. The architect received his due reward so everyone was happy. Except Amata and Basilio who were now penniless and had to become beggars in order to eat.

The message is ...

It makes more sense to plan before beginning a job than it does to spend time regretting failure later.

Songs

You've got to move	*Come & Praise* 107
Do your best	*Every Colour* 48
The building song	*Alleluya* 59

A thought to share

Do you think God planned the Universe?

Are you listening, God?

Father of us all, help us to plan for the future but let us never forget that there is always something to do today.

Lord, teach us to be thinking people who do not always have to be told the right thing to do.

Dear God, we shall have this day only once. Help us not to waste it.

56
The matter in hand

Theme

Concentration. It is a well-established fact that children concentrate best when they are interested in what they are doing.

Starters

1 How many of you like a background of music when you are doing a chore?
2 Does it help you to do your work better? Why?
3 How many of you like to have the TV on when you are doing a chore?
4 Does that help you to do your work better? Why?
5 Who thinks that a background of music or TV helps you to do your homework better? Why?

Story

Megabucks and sausages

'Now sit still, and concentrate while I tell you this strange story,' said Aunt Ermyntrude, putting down her teacup. 'You can believe it or not, as you please.'

She began … 'All Edward Grasper ever wanted was to be a rich man. He spent all his time trying to make money, usually without much success. One day, as he ate his lunch in the park, an old man came and sat next to him.

To his surprise, the old man spoke to him. 'You would like to be rich, wouldn't you, Edgar? Supposing I tell you how to do become wealthy?'

'How do you know my name? What do I have to do? And what's in it for you?' asked Edgar.

The little old man sighed. 'Oh, nothing in it for me, except to know that I am doing a favour for an ambitious young man. Just as I was, long ago.'

He whispered in Edgar's ear, 'This is what you do. If someone comes to you with an idea for making money just say, "Megabucks" to yourself – or other people will think you are mad. A little voice will whisper in your ear, "Good deal" if the idea is good.'

'What's the catch?' said Edgar.

'No catch,' whispered the little old man. Just *concentrate* on the voice in your ear and nothing else. If, however, you lose your concentration just a fraction, or you think even once of the word "Sausages", you will *not* be able to rely on what the voice says. That is the catch. You *must* concentrate on the voice and close your mind to everything else. It's difficult, I know, but it can be done.'

Edgar opened his mouth to ask a question but his companion had gone. Next day, as he walked through the local market he bumped into an old friend, who offered him five thousand shiny balloons, very cheaply. Feeling like a complete idiot, Edgar turned away and muttered 'Megabucks'.

He was amazed when a squeaky little voice *did* whisper in his ear, 'Good deal'. What is more, Edgar was so busy concentrating on the voice that he never once thought of the forbidden word 'Sausages'. He bought all the balloons and sold them at the next carnival, making a profit of a thousand pounds. But, sad to say, for no good reason, the next time he was offered other bargains he could not help thinking of the word, 'Sausages' after he had said 'Megabucks'. He just could *not* concentrate on the business and the word 'Megabucks' and nothing else. And, surprise, surprise! No little voice squeaked in his ear, 'Good deal'.

Worse was to come. Every time after that, whenever he tried to concentrate on the word 'Megabucks', and nothing else, he could not help but think of the word, 'Sausages'. As a result, he never heard the squeaky little voice saying the words, 'Good deal' again.

And that was the end of Edgar's attempts to become rich. Aunt Ermyntrude poured another cup of tea, winked and said, 'You can believe this story, as you please. I don't mind.'

The message is ...

It is amazing what you can achieve if you concentrate on what you are doing and do not let your mind wander.

Songs

In the bustle of the city	*Come & Praise* 101
On a work day I work	*Every Colour* 24
Mysteries	*Tinderbox* 40

A thought to share

It is good to concentrate on the matter in hand but it is not wise to exclude the world all the time.

Are you listening, God?

Thank you, Father, for our school and for all those who help us to learn here.

Lord, give us clear minds, so that we know where we are going.

Teach us, good Father, to give our full attention to whatever we are doing but let us never be so inward-looking that we cease to care about others.

57
Reading and writing

Theme

The importance of clear handwriting. Too many children allow their handwriting to deteriorate when they reach their last Junior year.

Starters

1 Who thinks good, clear handwriting is unimportant? Why?
2 Who thinks good, clear handwriting is important? Why?

3 Who will try to maintain their handwriting style at secondary school?

4 Who thinks that computers will eventually make handwriting obsolete? Would the disappearance of handwriting have any consequences?

Story

Waldo and the prescription

This story is loosely based on a true incident that resulted in a fatality (Gateshead, 1995)

Waldo Higgle had either a headache, or painful kidneys, or sore feet, or sharp pains in his knees. He really had nothing wrong with him at all. He was a hypochondriac. Which means, as I am sure you know, a person who suffers from imaginary illnesses. It was three o'clock one morning when Waldo woke his wife, Ethel, to tell her that he was having a heart attack. It might, of course, just have been indigestion caused by eating cheese and pickled onions before he went to bed.

Doctor Snobe was not pleased to be dragged out of bed and he was quite rude to Waldo; but he managed to convince him that he only had indigestion. When Waldo had finished groaning, the irritated doctor wrote out a prescription. Waldo moaned so much that Ethel got in the car and went to find an all-night chemist. When she found one, she handed the prescription to the pharmacist.

Mr Podd was very tired and rubbed his eyes as he peered at the dosage – was that 500 millilitres or was it 50? Oh, well, the mixture was only harmless indigestion stuff so he wrote the label – 'Take 500 ml every four hours.' When Ethel got home, Waldo took a dose at once and fell fast asleep.

Next morning, as Ethel cooked breakfast, she heard a yell from the bedroom. She rushed upstairs but Waldo was not in the bed. He was floating in the air with his nose touching the ceiling. and resembled a balloon wearing pyjamas. Ethel shrieked with laughter but managed to call Dr Snobe, who, although very tired, enjoyed what he saw.

Between them, they managed to haul Waldo down on to the bed and to tie him down.

It was several days before Waldo returned to his normal size. I wish I could tell you that it stopped him having imaginary illnesses but it didn't. You don't believe this story? Well, how do you explain the fact that, the very next day, Dr Snobe bought himself a lap-top computer, complete with a portable mini-printer, so he never had to write any more prescriptions?

As for Mr Podd, he decided he was fed up with being a pharmacist and got a job inventing puzzles for a daily newspaper.

The message is ...

This story is not entirely ridiculous – mistakes have been made in the past because doctors' handwriting has been difficult to read. Nowadays, more and more doctors use computers to print prescriptions.

Songs

Travel on	*Come & Praise* 42
Use your eyes	*Every Colour* 11
Give to us eyes	*Someone's Singing, Lord* 18

A thought to share

It has been said that 'the pen is mightier than the sword'. (Edward Bulwer-Lytton, 1803-1873). Can you explain what this means?

Are you listening, God?

Lord, help us to realise that we should never be afraid to learn and to keep on learning all through life.

Give us the wisdom, Father, to use what we have learnt in the past and to build on our knowledge.

God, our Father, teach us that we are never too old or too clever to learn new skills and to acquire fresh knowledge.

■ HOME AND AWAY ■

58
Who cares?

Theme

Irresponsibility. Actions taken, with no thought for the consequences, can often bring about dire situations.

Starters

1 Has anyone here ever stood on a road bridge and dropped anything on to the traffic below?

2 Or put anything on to a railway line?

3 Do you know anyone who has? (No names!)

4 Why do you think people – because it is not just children – do such things?

5 What do you think about such behaviour?

Story

A dangerous game

This story is based on an actual incident in 1995 that resulted in the death of an elderly woman, although the object that fell from a tower block was a large piece of concrete.

It seemed to get hotter by the minute as the bored friends sat on the tower-block roof.

'Can't anyone think of anything to do?' moaned Peppi. Five heads shook in in unison. Then, suddenly, a flash of inspiration lit up Dodo's face. Without saying anything, he leapt up and rushed towards the stairs of the tower block. The lift was, as usual, out of action.

He returned ten minutes later, interrupting an argument between Greg and Nosher about who had the filthiest jeans. Dodo was pushing a battered old pram, a huge grin on his face. It did not take the eleven-year olds long to invent a game. It was not very complicated – two planks as a ramp up to the parapet, a run up the ramp with the pram, let the pram go and dodge out of the way as the pram came rolling back. They had a great time for ten minutes.

Then Dodo charged up the ramp, pushing the pram and whooping like a maniac. To his horror, the handle of the pram came off in his hands. The pram shot out of his hands and disappeared over the edge of the parapet, Dodo falling flat on his face. He was just getting up when the four petrified children heard the screams from the street below, followed by the sound of a car alarm honking loudly.

Nobody waited to see what had happened. They bolted like frightened rabbits, each of them hoping that the scream had not meant the worst. Next morning, they met in the park to exchange news. To their relief, no one had been hurt when the pram landed. It had plummeted on to a car, crashing through the sunroof, setting off the car alarm and missing a passer-by by no more than a whisker.

They thought it was very funny when Noddy told the others on whose car the pram had landed. It belonged to Cosher, the caretaker and their deadly enemy. But, they stopped hooting when Peppi pointed out that someone could have been killed. That would not have been at all funny. For anybody.

The message is ...

Never do things that might endanger the safety of other people as well as yourself.

Songs

Morning sun	*Come & Praise* 93
Because you care	*Every Colour* 31
A better world	*Alleluya* 60

A thought to share

Do something in haste and you may well regret it later.

Are you listening, God?

Lord, help us to grow into responsible people who value common-sense as much as intelligence.

Father God, make us aware that many of the things we do can affect others.

Father of us all, help us to do all the good we can, by all the means we can, in all the ways that we can.

59
Being like the rest

Theme

Fashion. Children like to wear fashionable things – clothing, footwear, badges and so on. But, as we know, fashion is fickle and each generation regards the other's tastes with derision.

Starters

Teacher: You will have to decide whether you claim to know anything about modern (juvenile) fashion or not.

1 What are the modern casual styles for boys/girls?
2 Does everybody like present styling?
3 Will you still like it in, say, five years time?
4 Are there any old styles which you think might return? (Some already have …)

This may link with National Curriculum work.

Story

Blue is the colour

'Where did you get this scruffy lot of slaves from?' sneered Lucius. 'I wouldn't give you two sesterces for the lot."

  'Captured in Britannia by the 23rd Legion,' grunted Marcellus, the slave-trader, turning as someone poked him in the back. 'Hey, what do you …' His manner changed, abruptly and he bowed to the Senator who had prodded him.

  'I want that one there,' announced the Senator, pointing at the line of dejected-looking Britons. 'The short one with the blue face. My wife wants him.'

The slave-trader's face sagged as he looked at the slave indicated by the customer. 'Are you sure, Magnificence? I am told that he has a very short temper. I would not recommend him for your household,' he grovelled. The Senator glared at the slave-trader and offered 50 sesterces for him, which Marcellus accepted, reluctantly.

Two days later, Marcellus was in the tavern, when he realised that something was going on outside. The whole street was agog, watching the parade of at least fifteen noble Roman women, in their finest gowns. There was nothing remarkable about this, but every single woman in the parade had a blue face, blue hair to match and all wore blue gowns.

Viola the fish-seller shrieked to her neighbour, 'I am told that the wife of the Senator Flavius saw some slaves from Britannia with faces painted with a blue dye called woad and she liked the look of it. What some people will do in the name of fashion, eh?'

Zona, the olive oil-seller, shouted, 'Doesn't she know those savages only paint their faces blue when they are going to fight someone! Still, if it's fashion with them as can afford it, then it's all right! Isn't it, Viola?' But the fish-seller was laughing too much to answer.

The message is ...

Fashion changes frequently. What looks great one day can look ridiculous on the next.

Songs

One more step	*Come & Praise* 47
Points of view	*Every Colour* 45
Where did you get that hat?	*Jolly Herring* 24

A thought to share

If you pluck a chicken all you have underneath is ... chicken.

Are you listening, God?

Lord, help us to remember that what we wear is of less importance than the way we behave.

Father, teach us that our appearance may be important to us, but that not everyone else may share our opinions.

Dear God, remind us that fashions come and fashions go and that none of them are as important as some of us like to think.

60
Nothing to do?

Theme

Boredom. The condition affects adults and children alike, usually because the sufferers do nothing to overcome their own negative atttitudes.

Starters

1 Who gets bored from time to time? Why?
2 Who can think of any ways of overcoming boredom?
3 Is it essential to have activities provided for you to avoid boredom?
4 If you think that boredom cannot be avoided without the provision of facilities, what would you suggest should be provided for children?
5 Does it annoy you when you hear older people saying that they had to make their own amusement? Why?

Story

Holly's holiday

Holly was utterly bored.

They had only been at Bracklington-on-Sea for four days and, already, she was calling it Borington-on-Sea.

'I'm fed up with this rotten beach,' she grizzled, 'There's nothing to do except throw pebbles. I'm too old to make sandcastles.' To emphasise her point, she threw her tenth pebble at a demolished sandcastle.

It was unfortunate that her aim was faulty. The pebble landed on the young woman who was lying farther down on the sloping shingle beach.

The woman yelped and sat up abruptly, glaring furiously in the direction of the thrower. Holly hid behind her Gran, who had fallen asleep in her deckchair. She need not have bothered. Her unintentional target got up and headed straight for the Tyler family.

Mum sat up and Father began to apologise but the woman waved away his protests and stood, expectantly. Holly crept out from the substantial shadow of her grandmother.

'Your daughter *is* bored, isn't she? said the young woman, smiling sweetly. 'I know how she feels. I've been eleven, too. Perhaps I can do something about it. Would it be OK if she came along with me?' she said to Holly's parents. 'Oh, and you can check that I'm not kidnapping your daughter. Ring this number on the mobile phone I can see there. By the way, my name is Miranda.' Dad muttered something that might have been 'We should be so lucky,' but he checked the information anyway, expressing surprise that the phone had been being answered by a butler.

Holly was whisked off to Miranda's sports car, too taken aback to protest. It was dinner time when she tottered into the hotel, her face wreathed in a huge smile. She had enjoyed a *wonderful* day, she told everyone who happened to be listening.

'Oh,' said her Mum, 'So you weren't bored, then? What did this Miranda woman find for you to do?'

Holly launched into an account of the day's activities. She had been introduced to the world of horses and ponies and all that they involved. After being shown what to do, she had mucked out stables, groomed and walked ponies and, best of all, had been given her first riding lesson.

'And,' she announced, 'I haven't been bored *once*.'

When the horsey sessions and a quick lunch were over, Miranda taught her how to cook doughnuts, after which they played Scrabble. Half an hour of that and they went outdoors to try a short burst of archery.

When they had played a brief game of croquet, they ran out of time. All these things were new to Holly, and she readily accepted a promise from Miranda that they should do more before she went home at the end of the holiday.

Mrs Tyler, who listened to Holly's account of her busy day in amazement, enquired, 'Did you enjoy it all, then?' 'Oh, no,' replied Holly, 'Not all of it. I didn't like the mucking-out bit, but after lunch Miranda and I made a list of interesting things a bored person could do. Not all of them interested *me*, but I'd like to have a go at some of them.' Sure enough, the following day, Holly began by splashing in the sea and, when she had dried herself, she began to collect sea-shells. While she was waiting for dinner, she wrote postcards to two aunties and three friends. After dinner she played tennis with her astonished Mum.

As she said to her Gran that night as she tumbled, tired and happy, into bed, curing boredom is really only a matter of making an effort and using a little imagination.

The message is ...

There is no excuse for being bored – you will be surprised what there is to do if you look for it.

Songs

To ev'rything turn   *Come & Praise* 113
There's so much pleasure   *Every Colour* 10
New things to do   *Tinderbox* 58

A thought to share

Have you ever realised that being bored is an awful waste of time that you will never have again?

Are you listening, God?

Teach us, good Lord, to make the most of our time while we are able to use it to the best advantage.

Father, show us how to overcome boredom and help us to put our energies to good and kind use.

Father God, give us lively minds so that we need never have to wonder how to occupy ourselves usefully.

61
Not everyone likes your music

Theme

Consideration for others. We live in a noisy world in which too many selfish people pay scant attention to the well-being of others. Loud music is a good example of this and one which causes a great deal of friction in a household and distress to neighbours.

Starters

1 Who has a music system?
2 How do you listen to the music? (eg earphones, with the windows closed, etc)
3 Does anyone ever complain about it being too loud?
4 Do you care? If not, why not?
5 Name a type of music you don't like.
6 How would you like being forced to listen to it? You wouldn't mind? What about at three a.m.?
7 If someone was playing such music and you couldn't stand it any longer what would you do?
8 Are there any ways to prevent people from playing loud music that annoys others – especially at silly times? (Environmental bye-laws – refer to your local authority)

Story

Osolo the drummer

These events took place, far away in the middle of Africa, many, many moons ago, long before the time when elephants became hunted only for their great tusks.

There, on the banks of the mighty Alzani river, lived the Ijonja tribe.

Now Osolo, who was the chief's fine young son, wanted nothing more than to be a drummer. His greatest desire in life was to be one of those who played the drums that talked and sent messages over the trees and plains to other villages and, at the times of the feasting, sang and pounded out the rhythms for the dancers that whirled around in the dust of the place of celebration.

His father, Esomo, was not pleased, because he wanted his son to become chief one day. Nevertheless, he arranged for Osolo to be apprenticed to Ugama, the head drummer who would teach him both the making and the playing of the drums and how to speak the language of the drumskins.

Osolo began his learning at once and he became most skilled. But he went too far, pounding on his drums day and night until he nearly drove everyone mad, for no one could eat or sleep in peace.

The village goats went dry, the chickens refused to lay and the buffalo, the giraffes and the elephants left the plains in search of respite from the non-stop noise.

Villagers stole the drums when Osolo slept but he made himself a new set and resumed his perpetual pounding. The spells of the witch-doctor, Mbembi, had no effect whatsoever.

Osolo's father tried everything – he suggested hitting the drums with sticks that ended in feathers but that was no use to the learner-drummer. As he pointed out, what is the use of playing drums that no one can hear?

Ugama the drum-master suggested building a special hut made of thick clay, but Osolo made so much noise that the vibration cracked the dry clay covering the framework of the hut. The clay fell off leaving no more than a skeleton of sticks. Osolo's mother persuaded his father to build a hut deep in the jungle where their son could go to practise, but the drumming annoyed tribesmen from the Okara tribe and they told Osolo to clear off or they would dispose of him and his drums. His father tried another part of the jungle, but the hyenas broke in and ripped the drums to pieces. The final calamity came when Osolo was practising a new drum message in yet another part of the jungle.

It was unfortunate. The message he was practising meant, 'My tribe wants a fight because you have called our chief a piggish, greasy, ugly old simpleton'. Osolo had not realised that it could be heard by the drum-master of the Ibepi tribe, Masuta. The next thing Osolo knew was that a ring of ferocious Ibepi warriors, wearing threatening war paint, was surrounding his practice hut. The glittering spears that they were carrying looked *very* sharp and the warriors gave the impression of being distinctly unfriendly.

They only went away when they saw he was just a boy and after he told them that his father, Esomo, would apologise to Ozala, the chief of the Ibepi, although the insult was unintentional, and also give him ten good cows as a gesture of goodwill. The arrangement of practising in the jungle was obviously not satisfactory – there were too many risks involved – so Osolo moved back to the village.

But the problem still remained – his eternal drumming began to drive people away from the village. If it had continued, Esomo would become known as the chief of the tribe with no people.

In the end – and there had to be an end – it was Kinti, his little sister, who made the talking drums go silent. She trained her two pet monkeys to steal Osolo's drumsticks.

If he laid them down for a second, the little animals would whip them away from under his nose. He made new ones, but they were stolen as soon as they were made. He tried hiding them but the crafty little creatures soon found them.

So peace was restored. Osolo's drumsticks were restored on condition that he played his drums for no more than two hours a day. In later years, he took over from Ugama and became the head drummer himself. But, at no time, did he play his drums, unless he was asked to. And he *always* knew what the drums were saying.

The message is …

Nobody should do anything that annoys other people unless there is a very good reason for it. Playing loud music is one of the things that annoy many other people.

Songs

A living song   *Come & Praise* 72
It's a great, great shame   *Every Colour* 44
Sing a song of people   *Tinderbox* 18

A thought to share

Have there always been noisy neighbours?

Are you listening, God?

Give us, good Lord, the wisdom to appreciate that other people have a right to peace and quiet.

Father God, give us the ability to be considerate and caring about the welfare of others.

Please show us, God, the way to be good neighbours, but not just to the people who live next door.

━━━━━━━━━━━━━━━ THAT'S LIFE! ━━━━━━━━━━━━

62
Total truth

Theme

White lies. The predicament of being absolutely truthful at all times, regardless of the effect that the complete truth may have upon some people.

Starters

1 Who can explain what is meant by a 'white' lie?
2 Who thinks there are times when it is better not to tell the whole truth? Or should we tell the exact truth at all times?
3 If it was discovered that you had a nasty illness and you did not know you had it, would you like to be told about it?
4 If you knew someone else had a nasty illness only you knew about, would you tell that person the exact truth?

Story

The whole truth

Every Christmas, Zinnia's Great Aunt Mabel gave her a box of paints and Great Uncle Octavius gave her a box of almond toffees. When asked whether she liked her presents, Zinnia always said, 'Yes' and thanked them very much. As her mother said, it was not worth upsetting the old dears.

One Christmas morning she went to church as usual. The vicar, however, was ill and the Christmas Day service was being taken by the new curate.

'At this time of giving,' he warbled, 'Let us make the gift of truth to our loved ones and be honest at all times.' Zinnia was impressed. Why not?

After church, Great Aunt Mabel sipped her sherry and asked Zinnia the usual question, 'Did you like your Christmas presents, dear?' Zinnia took a deep breath and said, 'Well, no, actually I didn't. I can't paint and I don't want to, anyway. And I hate almond toffees. I'm sorry but I feel I must tell the truth.' Then she ran upstairs.

'Well!' exploded Great-Aunt Mabel. 'The ungrateful child!' She marched out of the room. Ten minutes later, the family heard the coughing engine of their old Morris Minor fading into the distance.

Zinnia was given a long lecture by her father and grounded for a week. During the week, she could not make up her mind whether she had done the right thing.

On January 3rd a letter arrived for her. Inside was a twenty-pound note and a letter from Great-Uncle Octavius: 'Dear Zinnia,' it said, 'Please accept this small reward for your honesty at Christmas time. Because we left early, it enabled me to go to the Model Railway Exhibition at the Town Hall, which I have never been able to do before. From your grateful Great-Uncle.'

Which left Zinnia even more confused. Did she do the right thing in telling the whole truth and nothing but the truth? Or would it have been kinder to her Great-Aunt to have said the things that the old lady would have liked to hear. What do you think?

The message is ..

You will have to make up your own mind – one should always tell the truth but there may be times when it may be kinder not to.

Songs

I may speak	*Come & Praise* 100
On life's highway	*Every Colour* 28
You and I	*Tinderbox* 55

A thought to share

Is it true that truth is stranger than fiction?

Are you listening, God?

Help me, God, to be honest but help me, too, to be kind.

Father, although truth is precious, let us remember that other people's feelings are precious, too.

Show us, Father God, what is true and what is false and let us always make the right choice between them.

63
We can't all be boss

Theme

Jobs and their importance. Many people in humdrum jobs hanker after something more glamorous often forgetting their own contribution to society.

Starters

1   What job(s) would you like to do when you are grown up? (You will have to restrain them ....) Why?
2   Is the pay the only thing that matters in a job?
3   Suggest some jobs that are not well-paid but are well worth doing.
4   Would you like to do them? Why?

Story

Lighting the bonfire

The castaways should really have considered themselves fortunate. They were the only survivors of the cruise ship after it had foundered on the uncharted coral reef.

No doubt, once the news of the disaster reached civilisation, it would be regarded as one of the most dreadful tragedies at sea since the Second World War. But, instead of being grateful, six of the seven people who had been hurled on to the white beach had done little but moan about their plight since they had realised that they were marooned on this tiny, uninhabited island, somewhere in the vastness of the Pacific Ocean.

Since the sinking, all had been gloom and doom but one of the survivors, who was a US astronaut, had managed to persuade the others to build a signal bonfire ready to attract the attention of any passing ship.

Early on the eighth day, that same astronaut, Colonel Dwight L. Snitzer, rushed up from the beach to where the rest of the party were trying to break coconuts for breakfast.

'Hey, you guys, it's a ship, a ship!' he yelled, 'I'm going to light the bonfire.'

'Oh, no, you are not,' announced Eleanor Miller, 'As European Commissioner for Energy, *I* should be the one to light the fire.'

The Colonel growled, 'Look, lady, *I* have been to the Moon and back. That entitles *me* to do it.'

'Indeed, no,' barked Lord Woolwigg, 'I am a senior judge in Britain and *I* am the one to light the bonfire!'

'Not so fast' shrieked Barbie Booful, 'I'm the only famous pop singer here and ..'

Herbert Pelcaps interrupted her, 'Be quiet, you silly woman, as a surgeon I have saved hundreds of lives so I am more qualified ...'

'Rubbish!' bellowed Archie Spanner, 'I employ thousand of people in my ten factories. I should light that bonfire.'

Then a man with thick spectacles and very little hair waved his arms about and shouted, 'I am Heinrich Mass, the famous nuclear scientist and my knowledge is sufficient to blow up the world. Lighting the bonfire should be my responsibility. Is that not so?'

Everyone turned to look as a young woman in tatty uniform, a ships's steward and the only member of the crew to escape the calamity, coughed politely.

'No, Sir,' she said, sweetly, 'I am the one who is qualified to light the bonfire.'

Spanner, the factory owner snarled, 'You? You are not at all important. You are only a steward, a mere cabin maid. Why you should be the one to light the fire?'

The steward cabin laughed and put her hand in her pocket. 'I am the only one with any matches,' she said, as she walked down to the beach.

The message is ...

Almost all jobs are important and we do not always realise how much we depend on other people.

Songs

The journey of life   *Come & Praise* 45
Don't you think we're lucky? *Every Colour* 25
Work calypso   *Tinderbox* 23

A thought to share

A job always seems attractive when you haven't got one.

Are you listening, God?

Father, thank you for the chance to learn so that we may be better equipped for the our lives in years to come.

Lord, take care of those people who have no job and help them to overcome their difficulties.

Father God, give wisdom to those who govern us so that they make every effort to find satisfying jobs for all our people.

64
What a player!

Theme

Sportsmanship. The need to be a genuine competitor.

Starters

1 Who thinks that the only thing that matters in sport is winning? Why?

2 If you have no hope of winning, would you still want to take part? Why?

3 If the only way of winning is to cheat, would you cheat?

4 What other benefits do you gain from taking part in sport?

5 Would you cheat at sport in order to make money? (Some people have ...)

6 Do you think we overrate the importance of sport?

Story

The man in green

The archery tournament at the Michalemas Fair was well under way. Among the competing archers was a group of strangers, dressed all in green, who by the look of their bows and scarlet-feathered arrows knew their craft very well. The local favourite, Will o'Stowe, had been shooting well all afternoon, his arrows thudding into the gold circle time after time. His main opponent seemed to be the leader of the green-clad group and his accuracy was just as deadly as Will's. It was four in the afternoon when the umpire called for a break so that the two final competitors might prepare for the ultimate shoot-out. They retired to adjoining tents to make ready.

Fifteen minutes later, to a flourish of trumpets, Will and the stranger in green made their way to their marks. Attending the man in green was his huge companion who went by the name of John. Each man was to shoot nine arrows in groups of three, the umpire tossing a coin to see who would shoot first. Each archer took strike in turn and there was nothing to choose between them at the end of the shoot. So it was that the umpire decided that the archers should shoot three more arrows, but one at a time.

Will took first aim. Again, there was nothing to separate the arrows until the very last strike. Will's third and last shot seemed to speed fast and true until the last yard of flight. Then, before it struck the target, it dipped and hit the outer rim of the straw circle. The green-clad stranger, however, made no mistake. His last arrow hit true in the very centre of the gold. There was no argument. Will shook his opponent's hand sincerely and told him that he was the finest archer in all England. The man in green did not seem to disagree with this opinion but he smiled a secret smile.

The strangers' cart was well on their way home before the big man called John asked the question that was on his mind. 'You slipped a warped arrow in his quiver, didn't you? Crept into his tent during the break, I warrant. You cheat, Robin.'

The winning archer roared with laughter and said, 'Now that would be telling, Little John, wouldn't it? You should know that when there's money to be won, I don't mind making certain there will be only one prize-winner.'

Small wonder that John refused to speak to him for the rest of the journey for he was too honest a man to approve of such deception.

The message is …

Some people will do anything to win but that does not make them good sportsmen.

Songs

I may speak	*Come & Praise* 72
Stick on a smile	*Every Colour* 43
Shoot! Shoot! Shoot!	*Apusskidu* 28
Football Crazy	*Jolly Herring* 15

A thought to share

If you win a cup or trophy by cheating would you bother to polish it?

Are you listening, God?

We thank you, Lord, for sport and games and for the enjoyment that we get from playing together in our teams.

Father God, teach us to play fairly and to understand that winning is important but not at all costs.

Give us the wisdom, dear Lord, to understand that we should not take part in sport to the exclusion of everything else.

Help us to realise that, however good we may think we are, there may come a time when we can no longer take part.

65
UXB

Theme

Cold courage. For many years, in peace and war, men and women have done brave things without regard for their own safety. Those men who dispose of unexploded bombs (UXB's) come high up on the list of the bravest of the brave.

Starters

1 Does anyone know what a UXB is? We hear quite often about unexploded bombs, usually found when building work has been started. Where have many of these bombs come from?

2 How are these bombs made safe? Who does it? (World War 2 bombs are usually tackled by personnel of the Armed Services. Other bombs may be neutralised by a Police Unit.)

3 Would anyone here climb down into a hole ten metres deep and crouch there, perhaps for hours, attempting to make a bomb safe?

4 Who can give other examples of real bravery in other circumstances?

Teacher: What follows is neither a story nor a narrative. Rather is it a fictionalised account of an incident which resembles many such incidents that really have happened. Not all bomb disposal has been successful – there have been fatalities. It is also worth remembering that not all bombs date from the Second World War.

Story

A day in the life

The foreman waved his arms frantically, pointed excitedly down the hole and yelled at the JCB digger driver. There was something nasty down the hole. The driver soon got the message, the digger came to a squeaking halt and he was out of his cab quicker than you could say, 'Unexploded bomb.' Within minutes the building site was deserted.

Half an hour later, the officer in charge of an Army Bomb Disposal Unit looked down at a streaked black and brown hump that was sulking at the bottom of the ten-metre hole in the London clay. Captain Murray clambered down into the hole, to emerge fifteen minutes later. 'Been there since about 1943, about 2000 kilos, and the big brute is going to need delicate treatment,' he said, wiping clay off his hands.

At dawn next day, a group of cold, dirty and wet soldiers were dismantling the floodlights that had illuminated the dangerous work of clearing away clay and soil from around the bomb. At 0600 hours, the captain and Sergeant Mackie went back down the hole. Murray lay alongside the missile and put his stethoscope to his ears.

'Something's going on, Mack,' he muttered. The sergeant raised his eyebrows, saying nothing. This was his tenth wartime bomb and he was still in one piece.

'Wrench, Mack, wrench,' said Murray, sharply. Mackie passed him the special tool and lay still in the stinking mud. He wished he was back in bed. He must be mad, doing a crazy job like this. Murray grunted as something gave way. His arm was moving and the sergeant sensed that the officer was turning something. Then Mackie heard an ominous hissing sound.

This was it. No time to get out before the German souvenir claimed two victims. He hoped that the rest of the party had taken cover. The captain gave a sigh of relief. The hissing changed to a ticking sound. Then it stopped.

Murray worked on, demanding tool after tool from his sergeant who knew in advance what tool was needed. Just like a surgical operation, with two lives depending on it. A few hours ago, more than two lives were at stake. If the digger had hit the bomb ...

Then the captain sat up, puffing, holding a small tube – the detonator. Sweat was running down his face and neck.

'That's sorted,' he announced with a huge grin. 'Safe now. They can take this one away and steam it out. But that's not our problem. Let's go and find some breakfast, Mack.'

And that is all there was to it. Another day. Another bomb. There would be others.

The message is ...

There are all kinds of courage, whether cold and calculated or in the heat of the moment.

Songs

Spirit of peace	*Come & Praise* 85
Working together	*Every Colour* 37
Hole in the ground	*Jolly Herring* 5

A thought to share

Someone once said that courage is doing something you are afraid to do.

Are you listening, God?

Lord, make us as brave as our minds will allow.

Father, we thank you for the brave deeds of all those who risk their lives to help others.

Dear God, take care of brave people when they tackle their dangerous jobs.

66
With my own eyes

Theme

Seeing is believing. This assembly does not set out to teach anything but aims to make children think about belief, and whether one can believe anything without direct sensory evidence.

Starters

1 Who believes in UFOs (or any other controversial objects)?

2 If you do, have you ever seen one? Honestly?

3 If you believe they exist and you have never seen one for yourself, how do you know there are such things?

4 Who can suggest ways in which you can be almost certain that something has actually happened, or that someone else has actually seen something? (Film, video, sound-recordings, ie not hearsay or alleged witnesses)

5 Can we even take film, video or sound-recordings as being an absolute guarantee that an event took place? If not, why not? (They can be faked …)

Story

Half a potato

Author's note: This is a true story. How do I know? I saw it happen with my own eyes about sixty years ago. The teacher really existed but

I have forgotten the name of the boy involved so I have chosen another name at random.

'For goodness sake, boy. will you stop fidgeting about? Have you got fleas or what?' said Mr Price, patiently. He was a large kind man who taught a class of forty-three boys between eleven and twelve years of age and they were a pretty hard lot. But no one ever took liberties with old Price.

'My hands itch like mad, Sir. Got warts, Sir,' growled Tommy.

'Let's have a look,' said Mr Price. The backs of Tommy's hands were dotted with ugly, crusty warts, not a pretty sight. Several of Tommy's neighbours made noises of disgust until Mr Price glared at them and they shut up as if they had been switched off.

'You want to get rid of those, do you, boy?' he rumbled. Tommy did not seem at all confident but he nodded uncertainly.

'Right,' said Mr Price, 'Bring a potato to school tomorrow.' Everybody thought old Price was going potty, but they were anxious to know what would happen. Next morning after register, the teacher beckoned Tommy to the front of the class and asked for the potato.

Tommy produced a nobbly spud from his jacket pocket. Mr Price took a neat penknife from his waistcoat pocket and sliced the potato in two, lengthwise.

'Right, boy, hold out your hands, backs upwards,' he ordered. His patient did so and the teacher rubbed the potato flesh on to the crop of warts, using one potato-half to each hand.

He gave the two halves to Tommy, flesh side up and said, 'Now spit, once, on to each half of the potato.' The bemused boy goggled at his teacher in disbelief, but Mr Price nodded, so Tommy obliged. The whole class was hypnotised into total stillness by these strange antics.

Mr Price walked over to the window and raised the lower part. He crooked his finger at Tommy who walked over to the window. Then he said, with a perfectly straight face, 'Throw the two halves out of the window, one at a time, as far as you can. Make sure you don't hit anything.' The boy did as he was told then looked at the teacher expectantly.

Mr Price said, smiling broadly, 'They'll be gone by morning. Believe me.'

Next morning, the class could hardly wait for registration to finish. Excitement swept round the classroom but it was soon hushed when the teacher banged his cane on his high desk. Now you can believe it or not, but there was not a wart to be seen on either of Tommy's hands. He could not believe it. Nor could anyone else. Including me. But it happened. Nor did the warts ever return.

The message is ...

If you see it you are more likely to believe it.

Songs

When night arrives	*Come & Praise* 92
Use your eyes	*Every Colour* 11
Mysteries	*Tinderbox* 40

A thought to share

Where does the television picture go to when we switch it off?

Are you listening, God?

Father of us all, give us enquiring minds so that we may find out as much as we can about this wonderful world.

Lord, teach us to ask questions about things we do not understand.

Dear God, be good to me because the world is so big and I am so small.

67
The finger on the button

Theme

Making decisions. Most of us have to make decisions at some time or other but some decisions are much harder than others.

Starters

1 Who can think of a situation where someone has to take the responsibility for making a difficult decision?

2 Who can think of a decision that was made and did affect many people?

3 Was it a good decision or a bad decision?

4 Has anyone here ever had to make a serious decision? Why?

Narrative

'Little boy'

Teacher: Some comedian may make something of the name *Enola Gay* – you must use your discretion as to whether you refer to the name, but the subject is serious..

The pilot of the B29 bomber (christened the *Enola Gay* by its crew) called all personnel on the aircraft intercom. 'We are beginning our bomb run,' he said, calmly. 'When you hear the tone signal, pull your dark goggles down over your eyes and leave them until after the flash.'

Through his bomb-sight, Thomas Ferebee, the bombardier, could see the unsuspecting city, nine and a half thousand metres below the silver bomber. To anyone who looked up into the clear morning sky, the machine was no more than a glistening silver speck. The sea sparkled and the River Ota cut through the patchwork of green and brown, far below, looking like a map in an atlas.

The bombardier called that he could see his aiming point, the Aioi Bridge. The tone signal sounded and all on board pulled their heavily tinted goggles down over their eyes. Ferebee, his finger on the bomb-release button, hesitated for a moment. This single bomb could end the long and savage war against Japan. It was not his decision to invent the bomb nor to bring it here. But, as a bombardier in the US Air Force, the decision when to release the deadly cargo was now his and his alone.

He pressed the button. 'Bomb away!' called Ferebee. The bomb-doors opened and the three-metre long bomb, called 'Little Boy', fell away from the bomber and plunged from the clear, blue sky. Forty-three seconds after the bombardier pressed the button, at exactly 0815 hours on August 6th 1945, the world's first atomic bomb exploded above the Japanese city of Hiroshima. In one terrible flash, a fireball as hot as the sun swept across the city and a fierce wind blew down buildings. In seconds, Hiroshima ceased to exist.

A giant mushroom-shaped cloud of smoke and dust covered the

town and rose 8 kilometres high into the air, blotting out the bright morning sunshine.

The Japanese government claimed that 70,000 people had died in the blast. Many more would die over the next days, months and years from the effects of radiation.

A week later, on August 15th, the Second World War ended when the Japanese surrendered to the Allies.

The world had entered upon the the nuclear age, when the launch of missiles tipped with nuclear weapons could have meant the end of the world.

Happily for all mankind, this age, too, has passed.

The message is ...

Some people have to make important decisions. Some are more important than others but they still have to be made.

Songs

All the nations of the earth	*Come & Praise* 14
Every colour under the sun	*Every Colour* 16
Where have all the flowers gone?	*Alleluya* 37

A thought to share

It is important that, if we make a decision, we should do our best to abide by it.

Are you listening, God?

Father, as we grow up, help us to make decisions bravely if we know they have to be made.

Lord, give us your guidance to make the right decisions if ever we are called upon to decide on what has to be done or said.

Father God, be with us all through our lives and in all we do.

68
The window of my mind *

Teacher: You must consider your own school population before undertaking this assembly. Some children might find the concepts in this assembly disturbing.

Theme

Coping with paralysis.

Starters *(These are factual, rather than leading, questions)*

1 Who knows what an astronomer is? (Ultimately, one who studies the Universe.)
2 Who knows what a cosmologist is? (That's a hard one – they differ from astronomers in that they study the beginnings and nature of the Universe. They do not use telescopes of any kind but they try to work things out through mathematics and the science called physics – the study of energy and matter.)

Narrative

My voice is a computer

Can you possible imagine what it must be like to be completely paralysed? Not just unable to move your fingers and toes and arms and legs. Not just unable to turn your head. You cannot speak or laugh. You can move your eyelids. And two fingers. Nothing else.

Amazingly, there is one remarkable man, as paralysed as this, who is considered to be one of the leading scientists in the world today. His name is Stephen Hawking ands his science is cosmology. This is the science of ideas that deals with the mysteries of the Universe – what it is, where it came from and where it is going. Cosmologists use computers and their brains to work out their ideas which are expressed as mathematics.

They do not look at telescopes and they do all their research without ever looking at stars and planets. Stephen Hawking can only move his eyelids and two fingers on one hand to operate a computer that is his only voice.

He has not always been paralysed. His illness began in 1962. It is known as motor neurone disease. Since then, he has worked out ideas that have astonished other cosmologists and he has written a book called *A Brief History of Time*. It has been written in simple language so that people who are not scientists can understand what Hawking is saying about the Universe. Millions of copies of this book have been sold and it has been made into a film and video. You may even have seen it.

The book is not an easy one to understand, even for grown-ups, but, when you are older, you may read it and follow its reasoning. You should never forget, however, that what you read will be the thoughts of one man, based on mathematical calculations.

These new ideas, about the birth of the Universe billions of years ago, have helped scientists to understand more about how the Universe began. We should remember that they came from the brain of a very intelligent man who cannot move, nor speak without the help of a computer, and remember that even the most disabled people can do the most remarkable things.

The message is ...

Some people overcome severe physical problems in the most astonishing way.

Songs

The bell of creation	*Come & Praise* 86
My mind to me a kingdom is	*Every Colour* 18
The world is big, the world is small	*Tinderbox* 33

A thought to share

One's brain may travel on great journeys even though one's body cannot.

Are you listening, God?

Lord of the Universe, we thank you for the strength of our bodies and the power of our minds.

Thank you, Father, for the minds and wisdom of people like Stephen Hawking who add to the sum of human knowledge.

Father, show us how to be considerate to people who are less fortunate than ourselves even when we may find it inconvenient.

69
A new man*

Teacher: You must consider your own school population before undertaking this assembly. Some children might find the concepts in this assembly disturbing.

Theme

Overcoming the disfigurement of terrible burns.

Starters (These are factual, rather than leading, questions)

1 Who knows where The Falkland Islands are?
2 Who knows where Argentina is?
3 What has Argentina to do with the Falkland Islands?
4 Why did Britain go to to war with Argentina in 1982?

Narrative

The life and times of Simon Weston

The life of the young Welsh Guardsman, Simon Weston, changed for ever in five minutes of fear and pain on June 8th 1982. He was a soldier in the Task Force sent to drive out the Argentinian invaders of the British Falkland Islands in the South Atlantic Ocean, 12,000 miles from the UK.

HMS Galahad, a naval supply ship, was anchored off Bluff Cove, in the Falkland Islands. It was there that Guardsman Weston, aged 20, was to experience the devastating results of the dropping of a single bomb from an Argentian Skyhawk jetplane. The bomb ripped through the thin hull of the ship, causing havoc below decks. Fifty Welsh Guardsmen died, most of them Simon's mates, as the ship became a blazing inferno. By some miracle Simon Weston survived, although he was terribly burned.

In his description of the attack he recalls, 'The colours were so strong and I can still see them, red and orange. It seems like yesterday. The second it happened I was changed for the rest of my life.' Forty operations have been performed on his face, including rebuilding his ears and the shape of his eyes, but he is still very disfigured.

Simon set up a charity in Liverpool, called 'Weston Spirit', which helps young unemployed people He now lives in Wales with his wife and children. There, he has his own radio chat-show called 'Simon's People'. The ex-Guardsman is in demand to give what are called 'after-dinner' speeches and he has written a novel called *Cause of Death*.

Despite all that Simon Weston has been through, he says, 'I've got a lucky streak. I am able to inspire people and I'm no longer ashamed of what I look like, who I am, or what happened to me. I'm better than the man I was.' And how many people can say that?

The message is ...

Many people overcome the loss of limbs to make a success of their lives. They are to be admired but Simon Weston lost his face. For him to become a success, he needed a different type of courage.

Songs

The journey of life   *Come & Praise* 45
Do your best   *Every Colour* 48
Give to us eyes   *Someone's Singing, Lord* 18

A thought to share

One does not need to experience pain in order to be to be a better person – it only needs determination.

Are you listening, God?

God, our Father, make us strong to face up to the unpleasant things in life.

Teach us, Good Lord, that the way we live is more important than the way we look.

We thank you, Father God, for the example of brave people like Simon Weston. May we do our best to follow his example of helping others.

70
A lot goes up in smoke *

Teacher: This has to be regarded as a sensitive subject and the attitudes of parents may need to be considered before presenting it as an assembly. You will be aware that current statistics suggest that habitual cigarette smoking is much more prevalent among children under the age of twelve than ever before. This is a good enough reason to include it in an assembly book for Junior children, although it is a subject dealt with at classroom level in a variety of ways.

Theme

The inadvisability of smoking. The assembly is intended to reinforce, or to be a pre-cursor to anti-smoking teaching.

Starters

1 Who would like to suggest why people smoke tobacco?
2 Who thinks smoking is a good thing? (Any offerings might be interesting)
3 Who thinks smoking is a bad thing? Why?
4 What is the biggest problem that faces people when they make a habit of smoking? (Giving it up)

Story

A last request

King Nosmo* boomed, 'You are not a lost explorer. You are a spy!'
The man protested his innocence, but the King said, 'At noon, you shall be thrown into the fire mountain, Tibabdah. I am, however, a merciful king and you are entitled to one last request. Name it.'

Toni Nice hardly thought before he announced, 'I would like a last cigarette.'

The King looked at his court and everyone looked puzzled. 'Whatever is a cig ...ar ...ette..?' boomed the King. 'What sort of food is that?'

*Anagrams (of course) King Nosmo = No smoking
Toni Nice = nicotine
Tibabdah = bad habit

The prisoner explained, 'It is not food, Sire. First you pick leaves off a weed called tobacco and you dry them in the sun. Then you cut up the leaves into small, fine shreds.'

'Yes, yes, what next?' said the King, impatiently.

The doomed man continued, 'You put the shreds on to a piece of thin paper and roll it into a cylinder. This you lick to make the paper stick.'

'What do you do with it, then?' asked the fascinated King.

Toni smiled and said cheerfully, 'You put it in your mouth and set fire to it.'

The King said, slowly, 'You ... set ... fire ... to ... it? Then what do you do?'

Toni said, 'You suck it. Not the end you set fire to. The other end. Then you breathe in the smoke, deeply.'

The baffled King mopped his brow and said, 'Do you not cough?'

'Of course you cough,' said Toni, brightly, 'that's part of the enjoyment.' At that, King Nosmo began to laugh, and he laughed for a full five minutes.

'And what is this strange behaviour called?' spluttered the King.

'Why, great King,' said Toni Nice, who could not see the joke, 'It is called 'smoking'.' King Nosmo wiped his streaming eyes, as did the rest of the people in the Great Hall.

When he had calmed down, he said, 'It seems to me, that however you look at it, this 'smoking' is a case of a fire at one end and a fool at the other. Let this man go. He is obviously too stupid to be a spy.'

What a pity the smoker was eaten by an alligator on his way out of the jungle. Still, at least it was quick.

And the message is ...

As the man said, 'Smoking is a case of a fire on one end and a fool on the other'. Ask anyone who has tried to give up smoking.

Songs

You've got to move	*Come & Praise* 107
There's so much pleasure	*Every Colour* 10
Turn, turn, turn	*Alleluya* 32

A thought to share

Why is it that world champion athletes never smoke?

Are you listening, God?

Father, give us the good sense not to take up habits that will do us harm and offend others.

Lord, teach us to treat our bodies with respect.

Father God, open our eyes to the stupidity of smoking, so that we can realise the harm it does to people all through their lives.

71
Music, music, music

Theme

Different tastes in music. Most people prefer one kind of music to another. Indeed, what is melodious to one can quite easily be torture to another.

Teacher: For the purpose of the Starters, the two current 'pop' idols are fictitious groups called 'Sludge' and 'Utterly'. You will need to substitute current heroes but make sure you get it right, if you don't want to be regarded as a reactionary. Pop fashions change overnight ...

Starters

1 Who thinks 'Sludge' is the greatest group in the world? Why?

2 Who thinks 'Utterly' is the greatest group in the world? Which one and why? (You can, of course, use the same questions for non-group vocalists.)

3 What makes one group better than another? Is it the individuals in the group as people or their music? (This can go on a long time if you let it ...)

4 Does anyone prefer music that is not 'pop'? Can you enlarge?

5 Is music the same the world over?

The discussion can be followed up at classroom level.

Story

Sound preferences

Mrs Rudd had not had a very good day at work. Which might explain why she was in a foul mood when she arrived home.

'Jolene, turn that row down,' she bawled into Jolene's bedroom.

Her daughter turned off her CD player and announced, 'Mum! It's Starzoom Boyz! They're stupendous!'

Mum grimaced and said, 'That is just a ... noise.'

Jolene protested, 'What about those old guys called Rolling Stones you had on the other night, then? Now that was noise.'

Before Mrs Rudd could answer, her son looked into the room. 'Girls arguing again?' laughed Paul.

His sister snapped, 'Mum says Starzoom Boyz are rubbish.'

'Well they are,' said Paul. 'There's only one group and that's Sponge Squeezers. Your lot sound like they're hitting tin cans tied to a cat's tail.' Jolene threw more pillows and Mum and Paul left.

When Dad came home later, he said that there was nothing like Plummy Thinette's Country and Western music.

Auntie Flossie called in for a cup of tea and said that the only decent music was Bryan Smith and his Happy Piano. ('Who?' said Dad. 'Never 'eard of 'im.')

Uncle Spencer declared that there was nothing like a good Italian opera sung by Soppiano Blott, and Mrs Fish, who popped in from next door, reckoned there was nothing like a bit of good old calypso. Soon, everybody was yelling angrily that their own favourite brand of music was the only one to enjoy. Then Grandad arrived and shouted so loudly that all the music-lovers went quiet.

Then he said, 'Now then. This is how I see it. Me, I like a bit of everything – Beethoven, Beatles, be-bop, reggae and rock. All of it. But you should all understand that we have different likes and dislikes. Life would be very boring if we all liked the same things. And I don't just mean music.' With that, he sat down and poured himself a cup of tea.

The message is ...

Everybody appreciates different things, music or anything else and we should appreciate this.

Songs

Let the world rejoice together	*Come & Praise* 148
The world is such a lovely place	*Every Colour* 8
Sound waves	*Flying a Round* 59
Calypso	*Flying a Round* 68

A thought to share

Isn't it strange how people change their minds about pop groups so quickly?

Are you listening, God?

Thank you, Lord, for music and for the enjoyment we get from all kinds of music, whatever they may be.

Father, if we are given the chance to learn about, and to make, music, help us to make the most of our opportunities.

Father God, teach us that our favourite music may not be the choice of other people.

72
The root of all evil

Theme

The love of money. Does the acquisition of money make for happiness?

Starters

1 Who would like to win the National Lottery jackpot?
2 What would you do with the money?
3 Would you be any happier than you are now?
4 Do you need a lot of money to be happy?
5 Is life happy with no money at all?
6 What is worse than having no money at all? (Owing money? Bad health? Loneliness?)

Story

The fabulous hoard

Gomez and Panza had found it difficult to believe they had actually found the long-lost treasure of the Aycheks in the ancient temple, guarded by crumbling skeletons. There were jewels of all descriptions, and they were rich beyond their wildest dreams. At their camp that night, they talked about their plans for their new fortunes.

'I shall buy the biggest mansion in all Brazil,' said Gomez.

'Oh, a string of racehorses and my own team of racing cars, bright yellow, I think …' laughed Panza.

'A helicopter and a yacht for me' said Gomez, rubbing his hands. Then they both fell asleep.

A month later, they arrived at La Paquito where a dealer told them that they were now multi-millionaires. Gomez, Panza and the dealer adjourned to the hotel in town to to celebrate their good fortune with champagne, leaving their wealth in the vault of the local bank. The bottles popped open and they raised their glasses to the toast of 'Wealth!'

Suddenly, there was a rumble which became a roar. The barman yelled, 'Earthquake!'

They looked out to see the bank disappearing into an enormous hole in the ground.

As Gomez said, shaking his head ruefully, 'Ah, well, another day, another dollar. For which we should be grateful. We would never have lived long enough to spend it all, anyway.'

The message is …

Two, really, – 'Wealth is not everything' and 'Never count your chickens until they are hatched'.

Songs

Simple gifts	*Come & Praise* 97
	and *Every Colour* 39
Stick on a smile	*Every Colour* 43
O Lord! Shout for joy	*Someone's Singing, Lord* 4

A thought to share

Money is not a bad thing – it is the love of money that causes so many problems.
(New English Bible – 'Money is the root of all evil', – 1 Timothy)

Are you listening, God?

Father, although all of us need money, let us never regard it as more important than anything else.

Lord, teach us to be generous to those who are less fortunate than ourselves.

Father God, teach us the value of money – never to waste it on stupid things but to put it to good use.

PART II

Special days: Festivals and celebrations traditional to the United Kingdom

These assemblies are not framed with any particular year group in mind.

73
Traditional New Year:
January

Obviously, this assembly is unlikely to be held on December 31st or January 1st but it could be useful early in the spring term.

Theme

Resolutions at New Year. Making resolutions is traditional at the start of a New Year but they are usually broken in a short space of time.

Starters

1 What is a 'New Year resolution'?
2 Who made one this year (or more than one)?
3 Who has kept it/them?
4 Who has broken it/them? Why?
5 Tell us about interesting and strange resolutions made by members of your family.

Story

Mr Cockle's New Year resolution

Mr Ossie Cockle was watching snooker on TV, but it was not easy. The noise from the street outside was almost drowning the commentary. About twenty children aged between six and eleven were playing a game that could just be recognised as football. There seemed to be a ball there somewhere as the yelling, hooting mob charged up and down the pavement and all over the road, the ball crashing against a front door now and again. Then the ball hit the Cockles' front window, shaking the glass but not breaking it.

'Right!' screeched Mrs Cockle, 'That's it! Those kids are driving me mad with their silly game. Ossie, go and shift them. Now! And don't tell me they will take no notice of you. You made a New Year resolution to stand up for yourself. Well, here's your chance. Go and shift them.'

'Aw, Beattie,' groaned Ossie, 'You know what those kids are like. All I'll get is a mouthful of cheek.'

Beattie Cockle threw a cushion at him and heaved herself out of her armchair, 'Right,' she barked, 'If you won't move them little horrors on, then I will.'

She stormed out into the street, and Ossie turned up the TV so that he could not hear what was going on. Even so, his wife's voice came wafting through the window and he got up to see her shaking her fist as the children left the front of the Cockle house in a hurry, even if one of them was sticking her tongue out at Beattie.

She came back into the living-room and crashed down into the chair, saying in a disgusted tone, 'They've gone. What a wimp you are, Oswald Cockle. Call yourself a man? You can't even stand up to a few little kids. Your New Year resolution didn't last long, did it?'

Ossie sank lower on the settee, opened another packet of cheese-and-onion crisps and muttered, 'I can stick up for myself if I have to. I just didn't want to be involved with a lot of kids, that's all.'

Beattie's response was a contemptuous snort. Then Butch Beestoke, who lived opposite, began revving his Harley Davidson motor-bike. Mrs Cockle let out a yell of fury and rushed over to the window. 'That idiot has been making that noise with that dreadful motorbike all over Christmas and I can't stand it any more.' Her husband pretended to be watching a tricky shot in the snooker match. Beattie stamped over to the TV and pulled the plug out of the wall-socket.

'Hey, I was watching that,' protested Ossie.

'Is that so?' bawled Beattie, 'Right, now you've got another chance to keep your New Year resolution. Get up, go out there, be a man and tell Beestoke to pack in making that row. Tell him your wife is sick of his noise. So are you.'

Ossie opened and shut his mouth like a stranded goldfish.

'Outside!' shrieked Beattie.

'Oh, all right, then!' yelled Ossie, "I'll go and tell him now. Even if he is six foot six, weighs eighteen stone and he's a Hell's Angel. You can sit by the phone ready to call the ambulance.' He went out, slamming the door behind him. Five minutes later, Ossie came back, shaking like a leaf. The noise from the motorcycle had stopped and Butch was waving at Beattie, who was looking out of the window, with a huge smile on his battered, bearded face.

She said, proudly, 'Well done, Ossie. Never thought you had it in you.' Ossie tottered into the living-room and collapsed on to the settee.

'So what did he say?' asked his beaming wife.

Ossie mopped his brow and gasped, 'Said *he'd* made a New Year resolution to be nice to all his neighbours. Just as well. Because he said that if he hadn't made the resolution, he would have chopped me up and had me for his supper.' With that, he fainted and fell off the settee.

A thought to share

Nobody has to wait for a New Year to make a good resolution.

Songs

It's a new day	*Come & Praise* 106
This way, that-a-way	*Every Colour* 53
New things to do	*Tinderbox* 58
Osghogatsu (Japanese)	*Musical Calendar of Festivals* p 10

Are you listening, God?

Father, guide us in this New Year to do only those things that make us better people.

Lord, teach us that when resolve to do something we should make every effort not to break our promises.

Help us, Father God, to do our best in every way in the year ahead of us.

Poem

New year cinquain and tanka, page 211

74
Shrove Tuesday
(Pancake Day): February/March

This assembly is intended to complement classroom teaching about the festival and has no religious significance in itself.

Teachers in non-denominational schools may like to remind themselves and the children about the origins of the day. Shrove Tuesday is the day before the first day of Lent, Ash Wednesday, and commemorates Jesus Christ's 40 days' fasting in the wilderness. The day takes its name from the act of being 'shriven', an old name for making confessions. It used to be a period of fasting but nowadays, Christians tend to give up luxuries instead. People used to eat up all their tasty food in one big meal – very often in the form of a giant pancake with all sorts of eatables in it.

Our present-day Pancake Day dates from this custom.

Starters

1 How are pancakes made?
2 How are they eaten? With jam? Lemon juice? Something else?

Poem

The Great Pancake Race

The most famous Pancake Race takes place in the town of Olney in Buckinghamshire. People come from far and wide to take part in the race which is run from the church to the Market Square, with a pancake being tossed in a pan on route. The race has been held since the year 1445.

Runners ready, armed with batter,
The recipe won't really matter,
All are ready for the race,
Anticipation on each face.
Competitors on starting-line,
The going's fair, the weather's fine,

Arrayed in all their overalls,
The runners to the start are called.
Red-coated starter rings his bell,
The crowd encourages and yells,
Runners from the church depart
Tossing pancakes – pretty smart!
Joe Ruzzi drops his on the ground
It hits the road with squelching sound;
Annie Smidge has great technique
(She's been practising all week);
Hubert, chef at famous inn
Gets pancake stuck to stubbly chin;
A pancake tossed by Gilbert Snoddy
Amuses almost everybody,
It lands upon a garden wall -
Gilbert's not amused at all.
Some pancakes tossed just miss the pan
As only leathery pancakes can,
They land on nearby flower beds,
Or, for a change, on someone's head;
But skill and practice wins the day,
Yes, Lizzie Trinket knows the way,
She hurtles into Market Square
Cheered by the crowd assembled there;
Up to the tape the lady flies,
The light of victory in her eyes,
Success illuminates her face –
The winner of the Pancake Race!

A thought to share

Tossing a pancake has to be learned – like most other skills.

Songs

Sing, people, sing	*Come & Praise* 110
Changing seasons	*Every Colour* 6
Shrove Tuesday	*Harlequin* 9

Shrove Tuesday   *Musical Calendar of Festivals* p 25
Pancakes!   *Songs for Every Season* p 45
One, two, mix a pancake   *Junkanoo* 13

Are you listening, God?

We thank you, Lord, for days such as Pancake Day. Let us remember that days like this are not without meaning.

Thank you, God, for our food and for the means of cooking it.

Give us the wisdom, Father God, to learn all we can about our country and its ancient customs.

Another poem to read: 'You can't make pancakes?' page 211

75
Mother's Day:*
UK – March, USA – May

An increasing number of schools now by-pass Mother's Day for a variety of reasons, but the assembly might be useful in schools that still consider the festival has some significance. You will appreciate this may be a sensitive topic for some children.

Originally, and for many centuries, the festival called Mothering Sunday was celebrated in Christian churches and it is still a date in the ecclesiastical calendar. On the fourth Sunday in Lent, everyone was expected to attend their 'mother' church, this being the most important church in the area, perhaps a cathedral. Because families came together at this time, it became a special day for mothers but it had ceased to be an important day for most people in this country by 1939, when the Second World War started.

Mother's Day, as we know it now, is a festival that was begun in the USA in the 1900s. The idea was brought to this country by the American servicemen during the Second World War. People in the USA celebrate the day on the second Sunday in May. Like Easter and Christmas, the festival has now become a very busy time for shopkeepers.

Starters

1 Who buys present or flowers and gives cards on Mother's Day? Why?
2 Who thinks too much fuss is made about it? Why?
3 Who thinks 'Father's Day' is a good idea? Why?

Story

The second Sunday in May

Joe pushed his battered old hat over his eyes and chewed at a straw that was even drier than the dust that swirled around in front of the shack.

The pitiless sun had beaten down from the hard, blue sky for weeks and there was still no sign to suggest that rain was near. This was worse than last season. That had been bad enough with only a poor quality small crop to sell.

Small wonder that his Daddy wore a permanent worried look. It was clear, even to a thirteen year old, that harder times lay ahead.

Joe threw a stone at nothing in particular and muttered to himself, 'I hate being broke.'

He did not even look up at his sister, Ellymae, as she wandered across the shack boardwalk towards him.

'What you doin', Joe?' she enquired.

Her brother grunted in reply, 'Thinkin'. Jus' thinkin' about how hard up we are. We ain't had an allowance for months. I've forgotten what stickjaw toffee tasted like. And do you know what day it is in four days' time?' The eight-year old girl screwed up her face as she thought about it. Then inspiration lit up her face.

'Sure I do. It's Sunday,' she announced, brightly. Joe heaved a sigh. She could be so stupid sometimes.

'It's Mother's Day, dumdum,' he growled. Ellymae's big, blue eyes filled with tears as she had another pause for thought. 'What we goin' to buy Momma for Mother's Day, Joe?' she asked. Her brother groaned in despair.

Lifting his head from his hands, Joe grumbled at her, 'How can you buy things if you ain't got no money? Huh? You tell me that? Huh?'

Ellymae thought about that for a moment and suggested, 'We could sell somethin'. You got your watch that Uncle Abner gave you and even if it ain't made of silver you should get a few dollars for it. An' I can sell Trixibelle, the doll grandmaw gave me for my birthday last fall. I don't reckon much to that doll, nohow. She's real ugly.'

Joe did not hesitate. 'OK,' he said, in businesslike fashion, Let's get a lift into Forksville with Daddy. I know he's going to see the manager of Pickett's Bank. Come on.'

Mr Carter was too full of his own problems to ask his children why they wanted to go into town in the heat.

Not that their trip was successful – nobody wanted to buy a cheap pocket watch and the storekeeper laughed at Ellymae when she asked him if he would like to buy Trixibelle, even if he did give her a piece of sugar candy because she looked as if she was going to cry.

When Daddy had completed his business, they rattled home on the old truck. It was even hotter than when they had gone to town.

Arriving back at the homestead, the children flopped, exhausted, on to the tiny piece of grass that survived on the shaded north side of the shack. It was as they lay there that Ellymae saw the little plant with its tiny pink flowers. There was no way of telling where it came from or how it had survived the relentless heat. Neither of the children knew what variety of plant it was. But you can be sure that they nursed it carefully through until the following Sunday.

They got up at crack of dawn on Mother's Day. Joe picked the delicate little blooms, oh, so carefully, and Ellymae wrapped them in a piece of green tissue paper that she found in her bedroom. They signed the Mother's Day card she had made with her crayons and presented it to Momma at breakfast.

Momma could not speak. She was so overcome with emotion that she ran out of the room.

'I reckon she was pleased with her gift even though it was only a few little flowers,' said Joe, happily.

'Was she truly pleased, Daddy?' asked Ellymae, 'Was she? But why was she crying?' Daddy smiled at her. He seemed to find it hard to speak, too.

But he managed to say, 'Oh, yes, honey, she was pleased. Very pleased. And she was crying because you have both made her the happiest Mom in all the world.'

A thought to share

It does not take a great deal to please someone who loves you.

Songs

Love will never come to an end	*Come & Praise* 99
Sing	*Every Colour* 50
It is the day	*Musical Calendar of Festivals* p 33
Mama don't 'low	*Tinderbox* 21
Supermum	*Tinderbox* 24

Are you listening, God?

Lord, teach us to love those who love and care for us.

Father God, take care of our families and help us to give them no cause for concern.

Father, we know that our parents worry about us. Help us to be sensible people of whom they can be proud.

Thank you, Lord, for mothers and fathers who care for us and love us. Help us to do our best to repay their love.

Poem 'On Mother's Day' (Aileen Fisher), page 212

76

Easter: March/April

Easter is the most important time in the Christian year, and this assembly is not intended to trivialise the real meaning of the festival. The events of Holy Week are generally dealt with as part of Religious Education rather than in an isolated assembly.

As with Christmas, the majority of children, even at Year 6, still give priority to the secular aspects of Easter, especially when it comes to seasonal food. Hot cross buns – which are probably not founded in the Christian faith at all – are popular with people of all ages and children are no exception. Teachers, however, who celebrate Easter in its proper light as a Christian festival and require an appropriate assembly may find *Assemblies for Primary Schools*, by Margaret Cooling, of particular value (See Bibliography page 241).

Starters

1 Who likes hot cross buns?

2 How are they different from ordinary currant buns?

3 Apart from the cross, how are they different from ordinary currant buns?

4 Why do they have a cross on them? (Best followed up in the classroom)

Story

Top cook

'What do you call these ... these ... things? You have the impudence to stand there and call them ... Hot cross buns! They look like lumps of clay.' King Herbert the First spat out the bun and gave his cook the sack.

He stormed out of the Court, shouting, 'Find me a new cook. In time for next Easter. Someone who can bake me some decent hot cross buns.'

The Queen and the Lord Chancellor spent weeks interviewing prospective cooks and eventually they found one, Marcel, a foreigner from the little-known country of Cordonbleu. His dishes were delicious but Marcel had a dreadful temper and could not stand any form of criticism.

'I am ze master cooker,' he would bawl, 'Nobody shall criticise my creations, my works of art, unsurpassed anywhere in ze world. I know everything there is to know about ze cooking!' After a year when everyone was pleased with his cooking, especially the King, Easter came round again. Marcel locked himself in the kitchen and would allow no one in. After four hours, during which wonderful spicy smells drifted all over the castle, he emerged, bearing a huge dish of shiny buns which he bore to the Court, his head high and a smug expression on his face. With great pride, he offered the dish to the King. His Majesty took one look at them and threw them at Marcel, bellowing that he was to leave the Court instantly and never return. To make the point, he pelted Marcel with buns as he left the room.

'Why did you do that, Herbert?' demanded the Queen, 'They smell absolutely gorgeous. What's wrong with them this time?' The King picked up the remaining bun and threw it into her lap.

'Look!' he spluttered. The Queen took one look and burst into shrieks of laughter. Not one single bun had a cross on it.

A thought to share

Nobody's perfect.

Songs

Now the green blade rises	*Come & Praise* 131
Hot-Cross buns Musical	*Calendar of Festivals* p 36
Pace egging Song Musical	*Calendar of Festivals* p 38
My Easter Bonnet	*Harlequin* 16
It happens each Spring	*Harlequin* 15
Sing out an Easter song	*Songs for Every Season* p 51

Are you listening, God?

Thank you, Father, for the enjoyment of hot cross buns and other seasonal foods.

We are grateful, Lord for bakers who work at nights to bake us hot cross buns at Easter time and bread and cakes all the year round.

Let us remember, Lord, those people who have no food and would be grateful to share in the world's bounty.

Poem Russian Easter Carol, page 213

77
Traditional Harvest Celebration:
September/October

Starters

1 Suggest some things that are harvested – it does not have to be food.
2 What do we call a farmer who produces wheat and similar crops (i.e. cereal crops … an arable farmer)
3 Why is a good harvest important to a farmer?
4 Are all farm crops harvested in the autumn?

Narrative

Victorian harvest time

This is a potted description of a harvest-time in the 1880s.

In the fields where the harvest had begun, all was bustle and activity.

At that time, the mechanical reaper with long, red, revolving arms like windmill sails appeared on the scene; but it was still looked on by the men as a farmer's toy. Most of the work was done by a man wielding a scythe, a long handled cutting-tool with a long, curved blade, swung by hand. It was a tool only handled by skilled workers, because one mistake and a very nasty accident could occur.

The farm labourers did not dream it would ever be replaced by machines. So while the red sails revolved in one field and the youth on the driver's seat of the machine called cheerily to his horses and women followed behind to bind the corn into sheaves, in the next field a band of men would be sharpening their scythes and mowing by hand as their fathers had done before them.

One of the fields was kept for women only. There were only three or four, apart from the regular field women, who could handle a sickle, a smaller cutting-tool than the scythe. Often the Irish reapers had to be called in to finish a field because cutting with sickles is slow work.

After the mowing, reaping and binding came the carrying, the busiest time of all. Everybody had to move quickly, for when the corn was cut and tried it was essential to get it stacked and thatched before the weather changed.

All day and far into the twilight, the yellow-and-blue painted farm wagons passed and repassed along the roads. Big cart horses returning with an empty wagon were made to gallop like two-year-olds. Straws hung on the roadside hedges and many a gate post was knocked down through hasty driving. In the fields, men pitchforked sheaves to the one who was building the stacks on the wagon and the air resounded with shouts.

At last, in the cool dusk of an autumn evening, the last load was brought in with a nest of merry boys' faces among the sheaves at the top and, the workers walked alongside with pitchforks on shoulders. As they passed along the roads, they shouted:
Harvest home! Harvest home!
Merry, merry, merry harvest home!

Women came to their gates and waved. The workers were proud of their work; they were paid very little for it but they still rejoiced in their own work.

On the morning of the harvest home, long tables were laid out of doors for a great feast and, soon after twelve noon, all sat down to the good food and drink, the farmer carving at the top table and his wife with her tea-urn at another, the daughters of the house and their friends circling the tables with vegetable dishes and beer jugs, and the grandchildren in their stiff, white, embroidered frocks, dashing hither and thither to see that everybody had what they required. As a background, there was the rick-yard with its new yellow stack and, over all, the mellow sunshine of late summer.

It was a picture of plenty and good will.

Paraphrased from *Lark Rise to Candleford* by Flora Thompson

A thought to share

Food is not grown in the supermarket.

Songs

Pears and apples	*Come & Praise* 135
Now we sing a harvest song	*Come & Praise* 138

Harvest, harvest, come along	*Every Colour* 3
Look for signs that summer's done	*Someone's Singing, Lord* 54
When the corn is planted	*Someone's Singing, Lord* 55
Harvest song	*Songs for Every Season* p 14

Are you listening, God?

Thank you, Lord, for our food, for the people who produce it and for those who bring it to our shops.

Father God, we thank you for all the bounty of our earth, whatever form it takes.

Dear God, may we never waste food, remembering that it required skill and hard work to produce it.

Poem: 'Patterns in the corn', page 213

78
Hallowe'en

Hallowe'en is a festival that has lost, even to many Christians, its religious significance as the vigil of All Hallows or All Saints. As such, it is rarely celebrated in non-denominational schools. In recent years it has been actively discouraged from featuring in curricular work because of its links with witchcraft and pagan worship.

The arrival of 'Trick or Treat' from the USA, however, has revived children's interest in the trappings of the festival, if not in its Christian or pagan sense. Indeed, 'Trick or Treat' should be taken seriously because it is too often abused by children who do not always realise the alarm they engender amongst old and frail people.

Starters

1 Who knows what Hallowe'en really is?

2 From where does 'Trick and Treat' come?

3 Who goes out on Hallowe'en, 'Tricking and Treating'?

4 Is there anything wrong with that?

5 Can you think of any reasons why you should not knock on strangers' doors, anyway?

Story

Not a good idea

'Come on, Lester,' called Jaspreet, 'We're ready to go.'

The boy said, uncertainly, 'I dunno. My Mum doesn't like this Trick 'n' Treat stuff.' He walked towards the waiting group, all wearing masks – a witch, a gorilla, an alien and a couple of skulls. Lester produced his own mask and the group dissolved into howls of laughter.

Benny giggled, 'You can't wear that, Lester. Popeye won't frighten anyone, will he?'

'Oh, come on,' said Miriam, impatiently, 'Up to Markham Grange like we agreed.'

'I'm not going there,' squealed her brother, Harry, who was only seven, 'It's all dark and creepy and I wanna go 'ome.'

Jaspreet bribed him with a sherbet lemon and, eventually, they stood in front of the door of the big house, sniggering and pushing each other. Louise slapped Harry because he started to sing 'Away in a Manger'. Miriam hammered on the huge, black lion door-knocker and shouted 'Trick or Treat, Mister?' Then the Treaters-and-Trickers had the fright of their lives.

Instead of the front door opening, it began to glow with a weird, green, pulsing light. The children froze with fear. Worse was to come. Very, very slowly, the big, old, iron-studded door did open, creaking and groaning. The children watched, hypnotised, as the door swung wide open and they could see into the black tunnel of the corridor beyond.

There, more than blackness awaited. To their horror, a disembodied, glowing head with long white hair and beard floated towards them, a moaning sound coming from its open mouth.

The terrified group fled. All of them spent a sleepless night and it took weeks before the whole scary business began to fade. It was a week after Christmas that the same group went with a village outing to see a show in Carmeltown Theatre.

'Oo, look,' said Miriam, mouth full of popcorn, 'There's a magician on first.' The drum rolled and the compere introduced, 'Marvo, the Great Magician!' The stage darkened until it was pitch-black. Ghostly music floated from somewhere and ... the former Trickers and Treaters shrank back in their seats. A disembodied, glowing head with long white hair and beard was floating across the stage, a moaning sound coming from its open mouth ...

I wonder why they didn't go Tricking and Treating on the following Hallowe'en?

A thought to share

Not everybody shares your sense of humour.

Songs

A living song	Come and Praise 72
Because you care	Every Colour 31
Seeds of kindness	Every Colour 42
Jack o' Lantern	Musical Calendar of Festivals p 90
Hallowe'en Calypso	Sing it in the Morning p 17
Hallowe'en is coming	Tinderbox 35

Are you listening, God?

Lord, teach us that we should never have fun at the expense of someone else.

Father God, show us how to be kind and considerate people who will not disturb others.

Please, God, make us aware of what we are doing when we have fun by knocking at the doors of strangers,

Poem: 'Trick or treat': cinquain and tanka, page 214

79

Guy Fawkes Night

(Bonfire Night)

Many children give little or no thought to the origins of Bonfire Night and the reasons for burning a guy. Their minds are usually preoccupied with building and lighting the bonfire, letting off fireworks and eating seasonal food – and who can blame them for that?

At the same time, while the modern relevance of the Gunpowder Plot may be less than significant to many children, it is a part of British History, if not the National Curriculum. Besides, it is a story worth telling for its own sake.

This assembly is intended to complement the usual annual teaching about the 'Fireworks Code' and/or visits from the Fire Services.

Starters

1 What is the most important thing on Bonfire/Fireworks/ Guy Fawkes night? (safety)
2 How do we keep safe when letting off fireworks and lighting bonfires and during the fun?
3 Why do we celebrate Bonfire (etc) Night, anyway?

Narrative

In the cellars of Parliament

'It is near the time for Fawkes to set the fuses' said Robert Catesby. 'Soon, James the First, tormentor of all good English Catholics, will be blown to smithereens. The fifth day of November in the year of our Lord 1605 will be a day for all England to remember with pride.'

What good fortune that the plotters had found the cellar to rent, right underneath the Parliament buildings. The tunnel they had started to dig through the Parliament walls, three metres thick, would never have been completed in time for the State Opening of Parliament.

'Twenty barrels of gunpowder should be enough, I do declare,' laughed Thomas Winter, slapping one of his fellow conspirators, John

Wright, on the back.

'Yes, yes, yes,' cried Thomas Percy, clenching his fists in glee, 'Guido Fawkes stands ready in the cellar with matches and fuses. As that Scottish tyrant sits on his ill-gotten throne – Fawkes will strike and – Boom! James and his sympathisers will be no more.'

Catesby snarled, 'Tis all the Stuart fool deserves. He should not persecute those who would choose the faith of the only true Church.' The other twelve conspirators nodded and uttered their agreement. What they could not know was that they and their plot were already doomed. Lord Monteagle, a member of Parliament, had been warned of the plot by one of the conspirators, Francis Tresham, who was afraid that his own brother-in-law would die in the explosion.

Hours later, beneath Parliament, Guido, or to give him his English name of Guy, prepared to explode the gunpowder that was to send the King sky-high. Fawkes was about to strike his flint and light his match when he heard the sound of pounding feet and shouts echoed through the cellar. He stood, holding his implements of fire, trapped, betrayed. Two soldiers grabbed him and a King's officer held his lantern so that Fawkes' twisted face was lit up.

The soldier shouted, 'Traitor! In the name of the King, I arrest thee!' The unfortunate Fawkes was dragged away and tortured to reveal the names of all his conspirators. They were to die either when they tried to escape capture, or on the gallows, as did Fawkes.

On the night of November 5th, the subjects loyal to the King celebrated with bonfires. Someone made a figure of Fawkes from straw and threw it on the bonfire – and the same thing is still done today – with extras!

A thought to share

How many people who let off fireworks on November 5th know why they are doing it?

Songs

Guy Fawkes	*Musical Calendar of Festivals* p 96
The fifth of November	*Harlequin* 38
Autumn days	*Come & Praise* 4
Sing, people, sing	*Come & Praise* 110
Autumn	*Every Colour* 4

Are you listening, God?

Father God, we thank you for the fun of Bonfire Night and for the enjoyment that we get from fireworks.

Teach us, Lord, to be sensible and careful on Bonfire Night so that we do not annoy and offend other people.

Father, help us to make sure that our pets are kept safe indoors on Bonfire Night because they are easily scared.

Poem: 'Dad will be pleased', page 215

80
Not just for Christmas

Theme

Buying pets as Christmas presents

Starters

1 Who hopes to have a puppy, kitten or other pet as a Christmas present? Why?
2 What will happen after Christmas, and especially when the animal becomes an adult? Are you sure?
3 Some people abandon their pets after Christmas. What is the worst thing that can happen to them? And the best?

Story

Outcasts

'Why are you in this dump, then? growled the black labrador. She was talking to a miserable-looking little dog with short legs, a long tail and dangling ears.

Allsorts, to give him a name, whimpered, 'I have no idea. One day I'm eating expensive tinned puppy food and sleeping in a warm basket and being called 'Diddlums' and 'Koochy Poochy' and then I find I am wandering up and down some horrible road with no idea where home is.'

Jet, the labrador, put her nose up to the wire and said, 'These humans are so stupid. We give them loyalty and good company and then, when it suits them, out we go.'

'Were you dumped after Christmas like I was?' asked Allsorts.

'No,' said Jet, 'My owner went to live in a Council flat and had to get rid of me because dogs weren't allowed. And I'm not likely to be adopted by anyone. Unless they happen to like large, black, hungry dogs who need exercise every day.'

'Well, look at me!' whined Allsorts, 'I mean, look at me. Nobody knows whether I am a beagle, a bulldog or a bloomin' basset-hound. It was fine when I was a cute little wuffy-fluffy puppy but, as soon as I began to grow, out I go.'

The labrador sighed. 'Ah, well, that's the way of the world, I suppose. Humans say 'It's a dog's life' if they have to work too hard or they are badly treated. They haven't got a clue, lad, have they?'

'No,' agreed Allsorts, 'and someone ought to tell them that a dog is for life and not just for Christmas. But then they've been told that a good many times already. And they still throw us out when they realise we are going to cost them money. Shouldn't be allowed.' And he went to sleep.

A thought to share

Why don't parents dump children when they begin to cost them a lot of money?

Songs

All things bright and beautiful	*Come & Praise* 3
Take care of a friend	*Every Colour* 35
Pete was a lonely mongrel dog	*The Jolly Herring* 13
Digit the dog	*Alphabet Zoo Book* 10

Are you listening, God?

Give to us all, Lord, a sense of responsibility so that we care for, and about, the animals that depend upon us.

Father God, help us to understand that our pets cannot survive without us and that they need our love and care if they are to be contented and loyal.

Dear God, guide us so that, if we ask for a pet for Christmas, we realise that Christmas is soon over and we must care for that pet for the rest of its life.

Poem: Three haiku, 'Happy Christmas, Boofuls', page 215

81
A Christmas miscellany

The festival has become so secular and commercialised that, despite the efforts of schools and Christian churches, the real meaning of Christmas becomes increasingly lost to many people, child and adult alike. Younger children, through the offices of schools (not all of them) and Sunday Schools still delight in the story of Christmas, presented in dramatic form as Nativity plays, and older children still derive great pleasure from participating in Christmas productions with a Nativity/Christmas theme.

Children at an ever-earlier age dismiss Santa Claus as a myth and know full well what the truth is. But many of the cynics still hope he will turn up on Christmas Eve … secretly, of course.

No 'Starters' are suggested for this assembly.

All on a Christmas Morning: three Christmas scenes

You can, of course, read one or more during an assembly.

THE FIRST SCENE: SOMEWHERE IN WALES, C. 1934

The turkey

Money was short. In other years we always had a nice, plump chicken, a luxury in those days of hardship. But not this year.

Mam couldn't afford a chicken and was asking around to see if someone could get us a rabbit to roast. Then Dadda won the turkey in the raffle at the Miner's Club. Evans the butcher brought the bird round to our house on Christmas Eve. Mam gaped at it and gasped,

'It's like an ostrich. That will never fit in our oven! It'll have to be cooked in Billy Loaf's bakery oven.' That would cost two old pennies but many people in towns all over the country had their Christmas poultry cooked like that in those days.

On Christmas morning, bright and early, Dadda put the monster into a wash-basin he took from out of his bedroom. My sister, Gwenny, and I pushed the precious load round to Billy Loaf's bakery in our brother Davy's old pram.

'Come back at half-past one,' said Billy, who had a piece of holly in his baker's hat. 'Done to a turn it will be.'

Off we rushed home to play Snakes and Ladders, even if it was only seven o'clock in the morning.

Mam was up at about nine o'clock to get the vegetables ready and to put the pudding on to boil. Excitement was in the air but all we could think of was that lovely gobbler sizzling away in Billy Loaf's big oven.

Quarter past one came and we rushed over to the bakery, trundling the pram at full speed. But, oh, dear. Billy Loaf greeted us with a face as long as Father Christmas' beard.

'Don't know how to tell you this,' he mumbled, wringing his hands, 'but we had a little accident. The oven got a bit too hot. Your turkey's a bit overdone. Crisp, like. Very brown. Tell you what. You can have your money back.'

We crept into the gloom of the bakery. The turkey was on a metal tray on the table where Billy usually kneaded the dough. The turkey was not just a little bit overdone.

It should have been a beautiful golden brown and smelling of succulent juices. Instead it resembled a large lump of charcoal. I shall never forget the faces of the rest of the family when they saw it. Little Glenys asked why we were having coal for dinner. I won't tell you what Dadda said. Man didn't say anything. Not a word.

It tasted like burnt cardboard. With gravy and stuffing. But we ate it. It was either that or potatoes, swede and cabbage. With stuffing and gravy. Still, the Christmas pudding was nice.

THE SECOND SCENE : THE CONFEDERATE STATES OF AMERICA, C. 1863

Visitors

Another bang of the street door sent the girls to the table, ready for breakfast.

'Merry Christmas, Marmee! Thank you for our books!' the girls cried in chorus.

'Merry Christmas, little daughters! Now, not far away from here lies a poor woman with a new-born baby and several other children. Will you give them your breakfast as a Christmas present?' Because they were so hungry, the girls hesitated.

Then Jo exclaimed, 'I'm so glad you came before we began!'

'May I help to carry the things?' asked Beth eagerly.

'I shall carry the cream and muffins', added Amy, heroically giving up the things she most liked. Meg was already covering the buckwheats and piling the bread into one big plate. Soon, they arrived in the poor, bare room with no fire, a sick mother, a wailing baby and a group of pale, hungry children huddled under one old quilt, trying to keep warm. In no time, a fire had been lit and all of them fed, mother and children.

'This is good! You are angel-children!' cried the poor things, in their native German language. The girls went away very pleased, never having been called 'angel-children' before. I think there were not in all the city four merrier people than the hungry little girls who gave away their breakfast and contented themselves with bread and milk on Christmas morning.

'That's loving our neighbour better than ourselves and I like it,' said Meg.

Paraphrased from Little Women *by Lousia M Alcott*

THE THIRD : SOMEWHERE IN ENGLAND, C. 1935

Waking up on Christmas morning

A ten year old boy wakes up in the ear-nipping, teeth-chattering iron gloom of his icy bedroom and peers across the expanse of the icy eiderdown. In those days most children under twelve believed in Father Christmas.

'Crumbs! He has been. My quilt is all heavy and lumpy. Gotta be presents. I'll sit up. Crumbs, it's cold. Must feel this parcel. Too small to be the train set. The telescope? Can't be. It rattles. Boring old acid drops, p'raps. They're all right for ordinary days but not for Christmas! P'raps there's a bag of those chocolate coins in gold paper or a chocolate watch or ...

Dunno what girls get. Dolls and skipping-ropes, I suppose. I've even heard that girls have clothes for Christmas. Crumbs, what a waste. Crumbs, I'm glad I'm not a girl. Reach for the next parcel. Crumbs, it's cold. My fingers are frozen. Wonder what time it is? Wish somebody else would wake up. I wonder what time it is? Crumbs. The church clock. Five o' clock.

Crumbs, I'm hungry. It's hours 'til breakfast. I'll die of starvation and my Mam will come in and find there's a skellington in the bed. Crumbs, I'm tired ... '

A thought to share

Christmas means different things to different people and to some people it means nothing at all.

Songs

Go tell it on the mountain	*Sing it in the Morning* 8
Christmas shopping	*Alphabet Zoo Book* 18

or a Christmas carol

Are you listening, God?

Thank you, Father, for the joys of Christmas. Help us to remember that not everyone celebrates Christmas – either because they do not wish to or because they cannot through no fault of their own.

We thank you, God, for the hard work that our parents and carers put into Christmas for us. Teach us how to show our appreciation for all that is done for us and given to us.

Teach us, Father God, that Christmas is a time for giving as well as for receiving.

Poem: 'Afterthought' page 216

PART III

Special Days:
Festivals and celebrations originating in cultures not native to the United Kingdom

The festivals chosen as backgrounds to these assemblies have not been selected for any particular reason, other than the fact that they are prominent festivals or celebrations in their own context. A brief background is given as to the nature of the celebration. The seven stories are intended to be no more than an assembly activity that can be conducted at or about the time of the festival in question, so that any audience may participate.

The stories can be read at the time of any of the other, equally important festivals that are listed, although this list is not exhaustive. The assemblies make no attempt to teach about a particular faith, as required in the National Curriculum, this being more appropriate in the classroom situation. Assembly 85 (American Independence Day) is, of course, not religious in nature.

The assemblies will be more relevant if children already have a degree of knowledge about the festivals celebrated. The months quoted are those of the Western Christian calendar.

82
Chinese New Year:
January/February

The Chinese New Year celebration is of two weeks' duration and falls either in January or February according to the phases of the moon. It starts on the 23rd day of the 12th moon in the Chinese calendar, usually some time between 21st January and 19th February.

The New Year is regarded as a new start and gifts of sweets and wine are offered to a Chinese god, Tsao Chun. Special meals are eaten and children are given presents of money in red envelopes. It is a very noisy celebration with the letting-off of fire-crackers. A 'Lion Dance' is much featured, the paper-and-silk lion being manipulated by young men who collect money in red envelopes as it dances through the streets, and people call out 'Kung Hei fat Choy!' which means 'Happy New Year!'

The Chinese New Year celebrates the coming of a year that bears the name of one of twelve animals: Year of the rat; the ox; the tiger; the hare; the dragon; the snake; the horse; the ram; the monkey; the cockerel; the dog; the pig. It should be borne in mind, although the celebrations appear to be 'pagan' in character, they are founded in religious belief. Three ancient and traditional 'ways' of religion are still practised in China: Confucianism, Taoism and Buddhism, although not encouraged by the Communist regime.

Other major festivals in the Chinese calendar (lunar):

Ching Ming (March/April): Offerings are made to ancestors

Dragon Boat(June): Celebration of humanity, order and justice

Moon Festival: Mid-autumn or lantern festival

Story

Why the hare has a split lip

Although this story may be Chinese in origin (some say it is Japanese) it has nothing to do with the Chinese New Year.

A hare who lived on the south bank of the Yangtse River passed many hours in wondering what lay across the other side of the big river. But, being a hare, he could not swim and spent a long time, trying to work out how he could get across to the other side without being eaten by one of the alligators that lived in the river banks. But the clever hare had an idea.

He could see the head of an alligator peeping up above the water. Putting on his best hare smile, he said, 'O Alligator, O handsome reptile, O beautiful scaly one, do you know how many alligators there are in this part of the Yangtse river?'

The alligator's head rose a little way out of the water and it said, wetly, 'No. I have no idea. Do you?'

The hare shook his head and said, 'Not really. But I have heard it said that there are more hares on this bank of the river than there are alligators in this stretch of the river.'

'Oh, no! Not so!' protested the alligator. 'There are far more alligators in this stretch of the river than there are hares on the bank.'

'I bet you there are more hares than alligators,' carolled the hare, 'and I can prove it.'

'How?' gargled the alligator.

'You round up all the alligators you can find,' chirruped the hare, 'and put them across the river, nose to tail. Then I can run along their backs and count them as I go. See?'

The alligator swam off at speed and collected as many alligators as he could find, several hundred of them.

The hare danced up and down and said, 'Right. Get into a row, nose to tail and I shall count you.' The stupid alligators did exactly that and the line stretched from the south bank of the Yangtse to the north bank.

'Aha!' cried the hare, taking a deep breath, 'Now I can count each and every one of you!' And he jumped from one alligator's back to another, counting as he jumped. When he came to dry land on the northern bank, he turned and laughed so much that his ears and whiskers wobbled.

'Ha! Ha! Dear, kind alligators! It was so nice of you to let me cross the mighty Yangtse river on your scaly backs. That was all I wanted to do! I don't care how many alligators there are.'

Then the hare laughed and laughed so much that he split his upper lip and that is why, today, all his descendants have a split upper lip.

A thought to share

We should try to appreciate the customs of other people. They may seem strange to us but would they understand some of our customs.

Songs

New Year Greeting	*Musical Calendar of Festivals* p 15
Can't help but wonder	*Alleluya* 34
Chinatown Dragon	*Harlequin* 24

Poem: 'Dragon Dance' page 217

83
Holi (Hindu): March/April

Hindu children act the story of how Vishnu, the great Hindu god, killed the demon Hiryana Kashipa. Vishnu appeared as a man-lion, to save his follower, Prahlad.

The name 'Holi' comes from the name of Holika, a demon goddess, who tried to burn Prahlad to death but was, in turn, burnt to death by Vishnu. Prahlad felt sorry for Holika and named a festival after her – Holi.

Hindu stories are full of stark imagery and violent action which children enjoy. The following story is much gentler in character and has absolutely nothing to do with Holi or any other festival in the Hindu calendar.

Other major festivals in the Hindu calendar (lunar):
Rama Naumi, (March/April): Celebration of the 'Way of Rama', foundation of Hindu life
Dusshera (September/October): Festival of the female deity, Devi
Divali (October/November): Festival of light and the female deity, Lakshmi, wife of Vishnu

Story

The toad's warts

Long ago an old woodcutter lived in the Lushai Hills in India. One day he went down to the river to find a smooth stone so that he might sharpen his axe. As he sat by the river, honing his axe to a fine edge, a prawn popped its head out of the water and bit the old man's foot. He was so angry that he chopped down the nearest tree, which was so upset that it dropped its fruit onto the back of a chicken that was scratching for seed.

The chicken was angry and scratched up an ants' nest. The ants stung a snake which bit a wild pig which, being in much pain, rooted up a Pukpuk tree. Sleeping in the Pukpuk tree was a sparrow which was so frightened that he flew hither and thither and ended up inside an elephant's ear. The sparrow tickled the elephant's ear so much that the elephant rushed around, knocking over trees, one of which rolled down a hill and flattened an old woman's hut.

The old woman told the elephant that he would have to pay for the damage. But he blamed the sparrow which blamed the wild pig which blamed the ants which blamed the chicken which blamed the tree that had dropped its fruit. Of course, the tree blamed the woodcutter who blamed ... of course! The prawn!

After much argument as to how the prawn should be punished, the animals held a trial and the prawn was sentenced to be boiled. A toad, who happened to live near by, put the prawn into a pot of boiling water.

Every time the toad lifted up the lid of the pot to see if the prawn was cooked he said to the others, 'Too much water,' and she drank a little drop to make the water boil more quickly.

The animals crowded round the pot, crying, 'Is he done yet, Mistress Toad? Is he done?'

Mistress Toad peered inside the pot but oh! calamity! The pot was empty.

'Oh, dear', croaked Mrs Toad, 'My mouth is so large I must have swallowed the prawn by accident!'

The other animals were so infuriated that they attacked Mistress Toad and pinched her and pinched her. They pinched her so much that skin on her back stood up like a lot of warts. And, ever since, all toads have had warts on their backs.

A thought to share

Stories can be funny, whatever part of the world they come from.

Songs

Hari Krishna Musical	*Calendar of Festivals* p 93
I belong to a family	*Sing it in the Morning* 3
Here's joy	*Sing it in the Morning* 31
Every colour under the sun	*Every Colour* 16

Poem: 'Holi' page 218

84
Jewish Passover: March/April

Passover is the most important Jewish festival and has, for hundreds of years, celebrated the time when Moses led the Jewish people out of slavery in Egypt.

For many years, the Jews had lived as slaves in Egypt; and Moses, who had become their leader, asked God to help him to lead his people to freedom in the promised land of Israel.

Jewish people eat special food and drink four glasses of wine during the Passover meal, which is the most important part of the whole festival, although stories from the Book of Exodus are told and there are questions for the children to answer.

Other major festivals in the Jewish calendar (lunar):
Purim (February/March): celebrates the deliverance of the Jews from a plot by Haman
Rosh Hashanah and Yom Kippur(September/October): Jewish New Year and Festival of Repentance, ending in a fast day
Sukkot (September/October): Feast of the Tabernacles, recalling the journeys through the wilderness

The following story has no origins in Jewish folklore nor in any aspect of the faith but its inspiration is obvious.

Story

The tenth commandment

The tenth commandment in the Book of Exodus says: 'You shall not covet your neighbour's house, you shall not covet your neighbour's wife, his slave, his slave-girl, his ox, his ass, or anything that belongs to him.' This commandment dates back thousands of years, but the word 'covet' still means 'I wish I had those things belonging to someone else – and I want them very much and I want them now.' This story is about just that.

Sarah Minchin peeped through the net curtains and almost exploded with envy.

'I do not believe it!' she protested. 'The Weebles have got another new car. That makes three this year!' Hughie looked over his wife's plump shoulder at the glistening new BMW, his eyes wide with disbelief.

'This is quite ridiculous,' he puffed, 'they've had double-glazing installed, a swimming pool built, their driveway replaced with that fancy block-paving and they've been to Thailand on holiday. Bertie Weeble must have got a fabulous new job to be able to afford all that since last August. I thought he was only a bus-driver.'

Sarah snapped at her husband, 'Why can't you get a job like that, instead of working in that dreadful old office for a pittance?'

'I reckon they've won the lottery,' grizzled Hughie.

"That's not the point. All I know is that I wish I was rich like them,' she said, tearfully.

'Doesn't seem fair, does it?' moaned Hughie. 'That we have so little and they have so much.' The evening dragged on until it was time for bed.

They were woken up at three a.m. by a disturbance in the street. Sarah staggered out of bed to look out of the window. Cedar Avenue was full of police cars and flashing blue lights and, as they watched, Bertie Weeble and his wife, Myrtle, handcuffed, were pushed into a police car. Sarah fell on the bed, kicking her legs and shrieking with delight.

'Now we know, now we know!' she yelled, 'Weeble is a burglar! And I don't envy him one little bit!' With that, she gave Hughie a big, fat, juicy kiss and went downstairs to make a cup of tea.

A thought to share

Don't just wish you had something – get out and do something to earn it. Just be sure you do not pay too high a price.

Songs

Shalom	*Alleluya* 76
Hava Nagilah	*Musical Calendar of Festivals* p 49
Sing	*Every Colour* 50
Here's joy	*Sing it in the Morning* 31

Poems: 'Seder cinquain' and 'Seder', page 219

84
Lailat ul-Qadr (Islam):
May/June

Muslims believe that Mohammed was the final and greatest prophet and that through him God revealed, once and for all, his will. The festival commemorates the night of power – on the 27th day of Ramadan – when the Angel Gabriel spoke to Mohammed, who was sent from God to give to the world the Q'uran, the Holy Book of Islam.

Other major festivals in the Islamic calendar (lunar):
Lailat ul Bar'h (April/May): The night of forgiveness
Ramadan (April/May – whole month): The long fast
Eid ul Fitr (April/May): The end of Ramadan
Eid ul-Adha (July/August – whole month): Pilgrimage to Mecca

The following story has no origins in Islamic folk-lore nor in any aspect of the Faith but is inspired by the Fourth of the Five Pillars of Islam which requires that Muslims give 2% of their income and certain kinds of property to charity or to the poor.

Story

You never know – do you?

Godfrey was very rude when asked to buy a paper flag to support the Lifeboat Society, known by its initials of RNLI.

'Push off!' he snapped, waving the flag-seller away, 'I'm never likely to need the services of a lifeboat. I hate the sea.' Being a sales-representative he had to travel a good deal and he always travelled by air or on land. But there is a first time for everything.

Godfrey was on a helicopter, flying to an oil rig in the North They were about halfway to the rig when the pilot said over the intercom 'We have an engine malfunction. Please put on your lifejackets and prepare to ditch. As soon as we hit the water, abandon the aircraft without delay and board the life rafts as soon as you are clear of the helicopter.'

He set down the helicopter on to the choppy waves with great skill and the passengers scrambled out and into the life raft. The pilot said cheerfully that he had transmitted a 'Mayday' message and the lifeboat should be here in a couple of hours. As they waited, Godfrey – or should I call him green Godfrey? – recalled his rudeness to the woman who was selling flags for the lifeboat service.

The lifeboat arrived to pick them up after the longest two hours of Godfrey's life, most of which he spent being seasick. Needless to say, he wished he had kept his big mouth shut when he was asked to buy a flag and wished fervently that he had bought one. His conscience told him that you never know when you are going to need someone else's help.

A thought to share

'Charity' is sometimes known as 'love'.

Songs

When I needed a neighbour   *Come & Praise* 65
Would you turn your back?   *Every Colour* 34
I belong to a family   *Sing it in the Morning* 3
With a little help from my friends *Alleluya* 38
Love somebody   *Tinderbox* 16

Poem: 'Ramadan', page 220

86
Independence Day, USA: July

On July 4th every year, the people of the United States of America celebrate their breaking away from British rule and the founding of their own nation, now the richest and most powerful country in the world.

Great Britain owned thirteen colonies in North America and the colonists objected to paying heavy taxes to Great Britain when they had little say in the government of the colonies. Their patience ran out and in 1775, the colonists, who were mostly farmers, fought the war called the War of the American Revolution. Supported by France, Spain and the Netherlands, they defeated strong British armies. The Americans declared themselves independent on July 4th, 1776 and, after several years of war on land and sea, the United States of America was born.

Peace was signed in 1783 and in 1787, George Washington was elected as the First President of the United States.

Independence Day and Thanksgiving Day (November)are the two main celebrations of the USA.

The following story has unknown origins in North American Indian folklore.

Story

Scarface*

In the peaceful years before the white man came with his iron tubes that roar and kill, there was a great chief of the first Americans, who were called, mistakenly, 'Red Indians'. This Apache chief, who was called Fat Buffalo, had a beautiful daughter and she was much admired by all the young braves.

None admired her more than a sad young brave called Tall Tree. He was sad because he had been an orphan since he was a child. His parents had died saving him from a savage bear that had attacked him. Tall Tree had survived but he had been left with a terrible scar that ran down one side of his face and made him very ugly and earned him the name of 'Scarface' from everyone in the tribe.

The chief's daughter, however, saw beyond the scar, loving him for the kind and gentle man that he was. They had spoken of their love for one another but the girl, whose name was Happy Flower, said that she was under a spell from the Sun God which did not allow her to marry anyone. Scarface resolved to journey beyond the Blue Mountains to find the Sun God. When he had found him he would ask him to lift the spell from Happy Flower and to remove the scar upon his own face.

He journeyed for many moons, climbing steep hills, swimming across wide rivers and braving wild animals until he came within sight of the Sun God's palace. Along the way, he found a golden bow and a quiver of silver arrows but left them there because they did not belong to him.

In a little while he met a handsome young man who said his name was Fleet Foot and he was the son of the Sun God. He asked Scarface whether he had seen a bow and arrows and, on being told where they were, went to collect them. He was grateful to Scarface and took him to his home, the palace of the Sun God. There, Scarface was made welcome and, the next day, he and Fleet Foot went hunting.

The young man's mother warned them to keep away from the Great Water but Fleet Foot was the sort of young man who enjoyed danger. 'Come,' he said, laughing, 'Let us have some sport with the evil spirits that fly like wild geese near the Great Water.' He and Scarface soon came across the evil birds and had to fight for their lives. Fleet Foot was so exhausted that he collapsed on the ground. Scarface fought on alone, shooting arrows at the birds until all his arrows were gone. At last he finished them off by wringing their necks.

When they returned to the palace, the Sun God was so grateful to Scarface for saving his son that he said to him, 'Ask any reward you choose.' It would not take a genius to guess what Scarface requested.

The Sun God said, 'Return to your own land. The woman shall be yours to marry, for you have earned what is dearest to your heart.' As he said this, the scar disappeared from the face of the brave. He was ugly no longer. He returned to his lodge, married the chief's daughter and was, from that day forward, known as 'Smoothface', little brother of the Sun!

A thought to share

The world would be a very different place if the Americans had lost their fight for independence.

Songs

America the beautiful	*Musical Calendar of Festivals* p 67
Battle hymn of the Republic	*Musical Calendar of Festivals* p 98
All the nations of the earth	*Come & Praise* 14
The family of man	*Come & Praise* 69
Home on the range	*Ta-ra-ra-boom-de-ay* 40

Poem: 'Independence Day', page 220

87
Dhammacakka (Buddhist):
July

Dhammacakka means 'wheel of truth' and celebrates the first day on which the Buddha (Prince Sihhartha, the 'Enlightened One,') taught the basic truths of Buddhism in his first sermon. The festival falls on the full moon day of the Buddhist lunar month known as Asahala. People visit the monasteries to hear the monks teaching about the Buddha and his first sermon. Gifts of food, often curries, and candles for the monks are brought to the temple.

Other major festivals in the Buddhist calendar (lunar):
Vesakha (Visakha,Wesak): May/June
Bodhi Day: November/December

The following story has no origins in Buddhist folk lore.

Story

The forbidden banana*

This could be a sensitive subject because it is an allegory referring to the use of alcohol and drugs, a practice that is abhorrent to Buddhists because the use of such materials clouds the mind.

The assembly can be used, as distinct from any religious association, to convey a message about the inadvisability of ingesting harmful substances.

Ozzie was a polite young orang-utan who never jeered at old or strangely-coloured orang-utans, nor did he destroy or damage trees or birds' nests for the sake of it. You might think, then, that Ozzie was a perfect orang-utan son. But I must tell you what is a truth for all growing-up boy orang-utans and girl orang-utans. They always know better than their elders.

Ozzie asked his mother if he could explore the dark side of the jungle. His mother said he could, so long as he ate no strange fruit and, most particularly, not the red bananas!

She warned him, 'Even one red banana can have some very strange effects upon a young orang-utan. So leave them alone.' Ozzie set off with his girl-friend Olive and, quite soon, they reached a glade in the dark side of the forest. It was Olive who spotted the red banana tree, the bright red fruit hanging down in great clusters.

'They look good,' she said, clambering up to pick a handful. She hung on the branch and threw Ozzie a red banana. He shook his head, saying that his Mum had warned him off.

'Oh, go on, Ozzie, don't be parrot!' (She had never seen a chicken) 'It won't hurt you.' She took a bite of the banana and it tasted really good.

Ozzie tried a mouthful. Delicious. His mother's advice was forgotten. They finished their first red banana.

They each ate a second one and a third. Then Olive fell off her branch. Ozzie found that he was staggering all over the place and wanted to laugh as loudly as possible. He found that his tongue was too big for his mouth and that he could not talk orang-utanese sensibly. So he started to sing, instead. Then he was sick. Olive giggled hysterically and fell on the jungle floor, kicking her legs in the air and whooping uncontrollably. Then she was sick, too. Suddenly Ozzie's legs gave way and he fell on the ground, too.

He remembered nothing more until he woke up in his own bed with his mother looking anxiously at him. He had a most terrible headache and his stomach felt as if an elephant had trodden on him.

'You stupid boy,' she said, angrily, 'We had to come looking for you. Now you know what the red bananas do to orang-utans. I did warn you. But you didn't listen to me. Thought you knew better.' Ozzie groaned and promised his mother he would never, never do it again.

But he did. I don't know why, because he was just as ill the second time. And the third and the fourth and … Because now, you see, he cannot stop eating the red bananas – he has become a red bananaholic. And he has only himself to blame.

A thought to share

People don't eat a lot of red bananas, do they? But they often put even sillier things into their mouths.

Songs

The journey of life	*Songs of Praise* 45
There's so much pleasure	*Every Colour* 10
Think, think on these things	*Someone's Singing, Lord* 38
Turn, turn, turn	*Alleluya* 32

Poem: 'Creatures' two haiku, page 221

88
Guru Nanak's Birthday
(Sikh): November/December

The teachings of Guru Nanak were the first steps in the formation of the Sikh religion, and Sikhs do their best to model their lives upon his example. The festival starts two days before the full moon in November by reading from the Sikh Holy Book in the temple. People eat vegetarian food that is provided at a free kitchen.

Other major festivals in the Sikh calendar (lunar, but some festivals are solar)
Hola Mohalla: March/April*
Baisakhi: April*
Divali/Diwali*: Oct/Nov
Martyrdoms: Guru Arjan Dev: May/June
Guru Tegh Bahadur: November
*Adapted from the Hindu festivals

The following story has no origins in Sikh folk lore but is inspired by the Sikh belief in the equality of all people, and differs from many religions in that women share in this equality.

Story

The new colleague

'Why, good morning, your Lordship,' said Norman Proddy, getting to his feet in a hurry.

Lord Lincoln, Chairman of Creative Designs Limited, waved his hand to suggest that the Assistant Sales Manager resumed his seat and said, 'Ah, Proddy, may I introduce you to Mrs Phyllis Poulter, who joins our little company from tomorrow. Perhaps you will look after her in the absence of the Sales Manager?' Proddy nodded, but ignored the hand that the smartly-dressed woman extended for him to shake. She and his Lordship raised eyebrows simultaneously and exchanged a knowing little smile.

Lincoln looked at his watch and said, 'Oh, I must dash. Goodbye, Mrs

Poulter. I hope everyone will do all they can to make you feel at home,' and left. The Assistant Sales Manager turned back to his computer screen as if the new colleague did not exist. She stood, waiting patiently.

'Well, don't just stand there, woman,' he snapped. 'Go and make me some coffee, white with two sugars.'

Phyllis did not move. 'Really?' she said, 'And what would you like me to do after that?'

Proddy heaved a sigh. 'Oh, go and file something or lick some stamps or something. You'll have to stand on your own two feet here, you know. You will have to show some initiative here.' Mrs Poulter's face looked as if it could shatter glass.

'All right,' she said, 'but first can you tell me the way to the Managing Director's office?' Proddy sent a wad of papers flying off his desk in confusion.

'Oh,' he said, sounding deflated, 'I beg your pardon. You must be the Managing Director's new secretary. I thought you were the new WP operator. Still, if you're going to work for the new MD, whom we haven't met yet, you'll have to pull up your socks. Won't she, Brimble?' His colleague across the gangway guffawed in agreement and lit a cigarette.

'Really?' said Mrs Poulter, in a silky, menacing tone. 'But I am not the new MD's secretary.' Proddy groaned.

'Is that so?' he said, sarcastically. 'I suppose you're the new Managing Director?' Brimble nearly fell off his chair with glee.

'As a matter of fact, I am,' announced Phyllis Poulter. 'And, from today, Mr Brimble, this is a 'No Smoking' zone. Good morning. I will find my own way to my office, thank you.'

A thought to share

Thinking that women are inferior to men could be a very serious mistake. In fact, never underrate anyone.

Songs

It's a new day	*Come & Praise* 106
On life's highway	*Every Colour* 28
Just the same	*Songs for Every Day* p 16
Both sides now	*Alleluya* 33

Poem: sonnet 'I am but a lowly scorpion', page 222

APPENDICES

A School Creed

Appendix I:

Poems for special occasions

Assembly 73:
Traditional New Year

New year cinquain

Midnight,
Now tongues of bells
Shout an iron message,
Come close the old book, open new,
New Year.

New year tanka

This resolution
I am resolved to keep
Firmly, at least until
Tomorrow or the next day,
Whichever may be the sooner.

Assembly 74:
Shrove Tuesday (pancake day)

You can't make pancakes?

Oh, it really does not matter
If you can't mix a bowl of batter;

Don't know amounts of flour,
Should the milk be fresh or sour?
If you cannot choose a pan,
At least you've done the best you can;
And as for tossing pancakes, well,
If you drop one, I won't tell;
Or that you have a good excuse
Because there is no lemon juice;
You can't find a cookery book?
So admit you're not a cook;
Another option you must find,
I'm sure nobody will mind
If you go to the baker's shop and buy
At least a dozen pancakes …

Assembly 75:
Mother's day

On Mother's Day

On Mother's Day we got up first
so full of plans we almost burst.
We started breakfast right away
as our surprise for Mother's Day.
We picked some flowers, then hurried back
to make the coffee – rather black.
We wrapped our gifts and wrote a card
and boiled the eggs – a little hard.
And then we sang a serenade,
which burned the toast, I am afraid.
But Mother said, amidst our cheers,
'Oh, what a big surprise, my dears.
I've not had such a treat in years.'
And she was smiling to her ears!

Aileen Fisher

Assembly 76:
Easter

Russian Easter carol

Easter eggs! Easter eggs!
Give to him that begs!
For Christ the Lord is arisen.

To the poor, open door,
something give them from your store!
For Christ the Lord is arisen.

Those who hoard, can't afford –
moth and rust their reward!
For Christ the Lord is arisen.

Those who love freely give –
long and well may they live!
For Christ the Lord is arisen.

Eastertide, like a bride,
comes, and won't be denied.
For Christ the Lord is arisen.

Traditional, from *The Lion Easter Book*
compiled by Mary Batchelor

Assembly 77:
Traditional harvest

Patterns in the corn

Corn circles
Of infinite variety,
Strange patterns in the corn to see;

Energetic, concentric,
Geometric, eccentric,
Oval, circle, ring and key,
Outlines brooding mystery.
Weird, eerie, unknown source,
UFO watchers claim, of course,
From alien root they emanate,
Perhaps suggesting Terra's fate?
Perhaps a tractor is to blame,
Indulging in some childish game?
Such puzzlement, not understood,
So are they bad? Or are they good?
Corn circles.

Assembly 78: Hallowe'en

Trick or treat: cinquain

Trick, treat,
Take care, aware,
Where you direct your feet;
Knocking on stranger's door
Beware.

Trick or treat: tanka

Before you knock on
That old, faded door, just pause
And pose the question,
Need you alarm the old and
Frail? For just a bit of fun?

Assembly 79:
Guy Fawkes Night (Bonfire Night)

Dad will be pleased

Choke smoke leaps up, and spirals, swirls.
Delighting noisy boys and girls
They all appreciate my Guy,
Who sags and slumps as sparks fly high;
But he is wearing my Dad's vest
And his old tweed jacket (not his best);
I wish that I had asked him first –
Oo! Wow and Pow! Guy's sack head's burst –
My Dad is bound to say I'm grounded,
And think the punishment well-founded,
Because his favourite jacket's torched,
His gardening trousers truly scorched,
I'm sure that he is going to spot it
Demand to know from where I got it;
It's getting late, the bonfire's dying
And, because I can't stand lying
I think I'd better go to bed
No reason not to – Guy is dead.
And I reckon I will be when Dad find out …

Assembly 80:
Not just for Christmas

Three haiku: Happy Christmas, Boofuls

Oo, he is so sweet,
A gorgeous, cuddly puppy,
Happy, waggly tail.

Oh, that stupid dog,
It's always under my feet,
It will have to go.

One more abandoned dog,
Christmas gift rejected now,
Just a broken toy.

Assembly 81:
A Christmas miscellany

Afterthought

For weeks before it comes I feel excited, yet when it
At last arrives, things all go wrong:
My thoughts don't seem to fit.

I've planned what I'll give everyone and what they'll give to me,
And then on Christmas morning all
The presents seem to be

Uselss and tarnished. I have dreamt that everything would come
To life – presents and people, too.
Instead of that, I'm dumb.

And people say, 'How horrid! What a sulky little boy!'
And they are right. I *can't* seem pleased.
The lovely shining toy

I wanted so much when I saw it in a magazine
Seems pointless now. And Christmas too
No longer seems to mean

The hush, the star, the baby, people being kind again.
The bells are rung, sledges are drawn,
And peace on earth for men.

Elizabeth Jennings

Assembly 82: Chinese New Year

Dragon dance

Now all things are new,
Sweep floor, polish house, shine glass,
Brand-new clothes, fresh start.

Here comes the third day
Out go the red envelopes,
Ready for the Dragon.

He is in the street!
Bulging red eyes, hanging tongue,
Leap, prance, dance, puff smoke.

See the paper tail,
And terror mask all gruesome,
Firecrackers explode!

Now the Dragon's feast,
He snatches from the door-posts,
Eats red envelopes.

Assembly 83:
Holi

Holi

Under the full Spring moon
Lord Krishna
watched young Rada,
Her young beauty
delicate as pollen in the air.
A slim girl
in the slender light.
Krishna threw powder,
coloured powder
soft and mischievous as love
under the liquid moon;
through shadowed veils
her eyes danced.
New flowers bloomed
next day in Krishna's garden,
frail, graceful girls
dancing their stories
to the powdered bees.

Irene Rawnsley

Assembly 84:
Passover

Symbolic foods are eaten at the Passover supper, the Seder. *Matzah* is unleavened bread; *haroset* is a dish of nuts, apple and wine, mixed.

Seder cinquain – Plaint of a Jewish boy

Matzah
I do not like.
Egg, lamb, haroset, yes,
But Matzah bread just sticks to my teeth,
Must I?

Seder

Why celebrate with bitter herbs,
salt tears of still-remembered slaves
and (though there's time now
for less hasty ways)
this joyless bread?

The salt reminds us still
of parting seas,
and, though there's time now,
once was none;
whilst plague took
Egypt's eldest sons
we brought to safety
our firstborn.

Pass over, Death;
Pass over, Death;
Passover …

                                        Judith Nicholls

Assembly 85:
Lailat ul-Bara'h

Ramadan

The moon that once was full, ripe and golden,
Wasted away, thin as the rind of a melon,
Like those poor, whom sudden ill fortune
Has wasted away like a waning moon.
Like the generous who leave behind
All that was selfish and unkind,
The moon comes out of the tent of the night
And finds its way with a lamp of light.
The lamp of the moon is relit
And the hungry and thirsty
In the desert or the city
Make a feast to welcome it.

Stanley Cook

Assembly 86:
Independence day USA

Independence Day

Why lie abed when the sun's rising high?
Don't you know that today's the Fourth of July?
Two hundred years this happy morn
Our Freedom and proud Independence were born.
These states were united and a striped flag unfurled,
Now known as 'Old Glory' all over the world,
So put on your costume, join the parade
And march with the bands of a great cavalcade.
Banners, streamers and ribbons abound,

Marching bands, cheerleaders from schools all around,
Policemen, firemen and servicemen, too,
Boy scouts and girl scouts and a place just for you.
Come to the carnival, come to the fair,
Come to the rodeo for everyone's there.
There's contests and games of every sort,
Baseball, softball, all kinds of sport.
And when it gets dark and you're ready for bed
And the skies blaze with fireworks overhead,
You'll remember your history and think with a sigh,
'How's I forget it's the Fourth of July?'

Philip Gross

Assembly 87: Dhammacakka

Creatures: two haiku

Whether they be slimy,
Whether they be great or small,
Precious to us all.

Of all life thus take care
Bounty given only once
Or else – extinction.

Assembly 88:
The Birthday of Guru Nanak

Sonnet: I may be but a lowly scorpion

Irritated scorpion lifts angry tail
And warns the monkey as it lopes along,
'Take liberties with me and you will wail
And sing a soulful, sorry, hopping song;
Because you swing through branches high, take care
You do not tread without regard;
You may swing freely through the jungle air
But at ground level things may well turn hard.
Do not annoy me or my sting you feel,
Once poison barb has plunged into your hide
Sensation goes and numbness on you steal,
So understand that we who crawl have pride,
Have caution where you put your simian feet,
I tell you, ape, a course you'll not repeat!'

Appendix II

Mood music

'Mood' music is usually played as children come into and go out of assembly areas and can affect the atmosphere of an assembly, although the degree of its influence is a matter of opinion. Some teachers would not regard it as being anything other than 'Muzak' while others believe that children of Junior age (Y3 – Y6) do take cognisance of 'mood' music. Schools with a music specialist, or a teacher who is musically knowledgeable, often 'post' the music for the day or week in advance and a number of children appreciate this. Many schools create their own assembly music through the media of school orchestras, individual performers – adults and children – and by invited musicians in place of, or as well as, 'canned' music.

Predictably, the most inhibiting factor in the selection of appropriate recorded music is the availability of resources. Some schools enjoy substantial in-school libraries, extra-mural libraries and authority or centre banks. Otherwise, teachers have to use their own collections and beg, borrow or … (well, this is an Assembly book …)

For that reason the specific tracks or songs can be no more than suggestions – many of the popular songs are being reissued as compilations on CD and tape and it is probably more useful to give the name of the artist rather than the composer. The pop music suggested is elderly but is still around and increasingly available as CD and tape compilations. Contemporary pop soon disappears from fashion and little of it can hardly be described as carrying a message. Classical music, too, is often most useful in the form of extracts from compilations. The list below only nibbles at the fringes of the world of classical music but, by and large, not many children enjoy 'heavy' music. Teachers, however, know their audiences.

Whatever form your musical atmosphere takes, it should, ideally, match the theme of your assembly. As you will be aware, this is not always practicable for any number of reasons, the most probable being lack of time to look for suitable music. If in doubt, aim for a calming background, or a 'happy' one, whether before, during or after assembly or meeting or whatever you call it.

Examples of tracks from compilations by major orchestras

The London Philharmonic Orchestra and the 101 Strings Orchestra on *The World's Greatest Melodies* (Alshire ALCD SPL-2)

Serenada (Drigo)	On wings of song (Mendelssohn)
Reverie (Debussy)	Estrellita (Ponce)
Etude in E major (Chopin)	Berceuse (Armas Jarnefeld)
Serenade (Schubert)	Romance (Rubenstein)

London Symphony Orchestra: *Classic Pops.* 'A Whiter Shade of Pale' (after Procol Harum); 'Paint it Black' (after the Rolling Stones); 'Sailing' (after Rod Stewart)

Vienna Philharmonic: *Strauss Waltzes*

'Popular' Orchestras and Instrumentalists that offer pleasant, neutral background music: Garry Blake Orchestra; Richard Claydermann (Piano); James Galway (Flute); Ron Goodwin Orchestra; Geoff Love Orchestra; James Last Orchestra. Mantovani's Orchestra; Jack Parnell Orchestra (esp. TV themes): Shadows (Guitars + Rhythm); Tilsley Orchestra (esp. TV themes)

More Specific Titles and Composers

Albeniz	Castillo (Spanish guitar)
Albinoni	Adagio for organ and strings
Anderson, Leroy	Sleigh Ride
Arlen	Autumn leaves;
Bach J S	Air on a G string:
	Gavotte (Spanish guitar)
Beethoven	Für Elise
	Symphony No. 5
	Moonlight Sonata
Berlioz	Symphonie Fantastique
Bizet	Carmen Suite No. 2 ('Habanera')
	Farandole from L'Arleisienne Suite
Borodin	Polovtzian Dances
Britten	Sea Pictures (Peter Grimes):
	Variation on a theme by Frank Bridge
Butterworth	The Banks of Green Willow

Charpentier	Fanfare from *Te Deum*
Chopin	Nocturne in E Flat
	Fantasie Impromptu in C Sharp Op 66
Copland	Fanfare for the Common Man:
	Outdoor Overture
Delius	Summer Evening
Dvorak	New World Symphony
Elgar	Overture Cockaigne
	Sospin
Faure	Poème
Fibich	Love's Labour Lost
Grainger	Country Gardens
Grieg	Homage March
Halvorsen	Entry of the Boyards
Humperdinck	Evening Prayer from *Hansel and Gretel*
Ivanovitch	Waves of the Danube
Orff	O Fortuna (from *Carmina Burana*)
Maxwell	Ebb Tide
Mendelssohn	On Wings of Song
Mozart	Eine Kleine Nachtmusik
Mussorgsky	The Great Gate at Kiev
Parry	Lady Radnor's Suite
Rimsky-Korsakov	Flight of the Bumble Bee:
	Scheherezade
Rubenstein	Romance
Saint-Saens	The Swan
Satie	Gymnopédies
Schubert	March Militaire:
	Serenade
Strauss, Richard	Also Sprach Zarathustra
Tchaikowsky	Chanson Triste
	Symphonie Pathetique
	The Sleeping Beauty
	Waltz from *Swan Lake*
Vivaldi	Spring (from *The Four Seasons*)

From popular films and musicals

Barnum	The Colours of my Life
Carousel	You'll never Walk Alone: The Highest Judge of All
Cinderella	A Dream is a Wish your Heart Makes
Jungle Book	The Bare Necessities
Les Miserables	I dreamed a Dream
My Fair Lady	The Rain in Spain
Oliver	Consider Yourself
Pinocchio	Give a Little Whistle
Snow White	Heigh ho!
Sound of Music	Climb every Mountain: So long, Farewell
Miss Saigon	Overture
Wizard of Oz	Over the Rainbow

Useful popular music

Most tunes have been performed by other artists.

Performer	Music
Abba	I have a Dream
Herb Alpert	Spanish Flea
Kenny Ball	March of the Siamese Children
The Beatles	Here comes the Sun; All you need is Love
Acker Bilk	Stranger on the Shore
Bing Crosby	Ac-cent-tchu-ate the Positive; Swingin' on a Star
Cliff Edward	When you wish upon a Star
Paul McCartney	Mull of Kintyre
The Move	Flowers in the Rain
Russ Morgan	Cruising down the River
New Vaudeville Band	Winchester Cathedral;
Whistling Jack Smith	I was Kaiser Bill's Batman

Tacticos & his Bouzoukis   Zorba's Dance
Tollefsen Hora   Staccata (Accordion)

Suggestions for music for specific assemblies

Most tracks have been performed by several artists

WITH YEAR 3 IN MIND

Theme	Artist/Composer	Music
1 Welcome to Year 3	Abba	Arrival
2 Adjustment	Tommy Dorsey	On the Sunny Side of the Street
3 A School Creed	John Williams	New Sun Rising
4 Paying attention	Mozart	Rondo from Horn Concerto No. 4
5 Monopoly	Dvorak	Humoresque
6 Taking advice	Julie Andrews	Superfragilisitic-expialidocious
7 School rules	Scott Joplin	Stoptime Rag
8 Teasing	Henry Mancini	It's Easy to Say
9 Too much TV	Cat Stevens	Morning has Broken
10 Cleanliness	Prima & Harris	I Wanna be Like You (from 'The Jungle Book')
11 Keeping late hours	Russ Morgan	So Tired
12 A lie is a lie	The Fortunes	You've got your Troubles
13 Acceptable table manners	Nat Gonella & his New Georgians	One Meat Ball
14 Telling the time	Haydn	Clock Symphony
15 Playing safely	Cyril Ornandel	In the Country
16 Reality	Nicola le Fane	Invisible Places
17 Talents	Johnny Mercer & the Pied Pipers	Personality
18 Overcoming visual impairment	Stevie Wonder	I Just Called

WITH YEAR 4 IN MIND

19	Absenteeism	Nat 'King' Cole	Straighten Up and Fly Right
20	Making excuses	Johnny Nash	I Can See Clearly Now
21	Litter	Louis Armstrong	What a Wonderful World
22	Saying 'thank you'	Bob Hope	Thanks for the Memory
23	Learning to swim	Debussy	Clair de Lune
24	Co-operation	The Monkees	A Little Bit Me
25	Cycling safely	Little Eva	The Locomotion
26	Over-indulgence	from 'Oliver'	Food, Glorious Food
27	Advertising	Julie Andrews	My Favourite Things
28	Orderliness	Gershwin	'Taint What You Do
29	Fire risks	Ambrose & his Orch	I don't Want to Set the World on Fire
30	Apologising	Bob Crosby & his Bobcats	Who's Sorry Now?
31	Fears	Jimmy Shand	The Bluebell Polka
32	Persuasion	Havergal Bryan	Trotting to Market
33	Beauty	Ray Stephens	Everything is Beautiful
34	Keeping promises	Coates & Lawrence	Sleepy Lagoon
35	Summoning help	Rossini	William Tell Overture
36	Overcoming physical impairment	Band of the RAF	Reach for the Sky

With Year 5 in mind

37	Lost property	Fats Waller	Ain't Misbehaving
38	Bullying	The Spinners	Family of Man
39	Reading carefully	The Carpenters	Please, Mr Postman
40	Owning up	Ives	The Unanswered Question
41	Standards	Shirley Bassey	Reach for the Stars
42	Class comedians	Grainger	Mock Morris
43	Versatility	Charlie Barnet	Skyliner
44	Graffiti	Tommy Dorsey	On the Sunny Side of the Street
45	Stealing	Widor	Toccata (Organ Symphony No.5)
46	Caring for pets	Semprini	Kitten on the Keys
47	Pocket money	Andrews Sisters	Money is the Root of All Evil
48	Computeritis	Shostakovitch	Symphony No. 5 (End)
49	Vandalism	Rossini	Overture Semiramide
50	Exaggeration	Jason Donovan	Any Dream will Do (from 'Joseph')
51	Honesty	Debussy	Images (Book 1): Reflets dans l'eau
52	Winning & losing	Mike Oldfield	Tubular Bells
53	Self-importance	Elmer Bernstein	Theme for 'The Magnificent Seven'
54	Overcoming hearing impairment	Sandy Nelson (or anything by Evelyn Glennie)	Let There be Drums

WITH YEAR 6 IN MIND

55	Planning	Bunny Berigan	I Can't Get Started
56	Concentration	Chopin	Fantasie Impromptu
57	Clear Handwriting	Max Bygraves	Lazybones
58	Irresponsibility	Busoni	Two Studies on Dr Faust – Sarabande
59	Fashion	Amen Corner	Bend me, Shape me
60	Boredom	Charlie Chalk	I'm Bored
61	Consideration for others	Bryan Adams	I Do it for You
62	Being truthful	Tommy Dorsey	Little White Lies
63	Top Jobs	The Beatles	Lovely Rita
64	Sportsmanship	Vienna State Orchestra	Acceleration Waltz
65	Cold courage	Vaughan Williams	Pomp & Circumstance March No. 1
66	Seeing is believing	Max Boyce	The Old Carmarthen Oak
67	Making decisions	Manfred Mann	5-4-3-2-1
68	Coping with paralysis	Dowland	Lachrimae Antiquae
69	Coping with disfigurement	Gracie Fields	Count your Blessings
70	Smoking	Phil Harris	Smoke, Smoke, Smoke
71	Musical tastes	Abba	Thank You for the Music
72	The love of money	Topol	If I were a Rich Man (from 'Fiddler on the Roof')

Festivals and celebrations

73	Traditional New Year	Abba	I Had a Dream
74	Shrove Tuesday	Ventures	Walk, Don't Run
75	Mother's Day	Richard Clayderman	People
76	Easter	Irving Berlin	Easter Parade
77	Traditional Harvest	Copland	Outdoor Overture
78	Hallowe'en	Dukas	The Sorcerer's Apprentice
79	Guy Fawkes Night	Handel	Music for the Royal Fireworks
80	Not just for Christmas	Any Christmas carols or songs	
82	Chinese New Year	Lyricord label	Chinese drums & music
		Decca	Chinese music
83	Holi	Copland	Appalachian Spring
84	Passover	Arion label	Songs and Dances from Israel
85	Lailat ul Q'adr	Sibelius	Pelléas et Mélisande
86	Independence USA	Bruce Springsteen	Born in the USA
87	Dhammacakka	Red Ingle & the Natural 7	Cigareets and Whusky
88	Guru Nanak's birthday	Argon label	Religions of India

Appendix III

Songs

Source books

1 **A & C Black song books**:   *Alleluya Apusskidu* (Year 3 & Year 4)
                              Flying a Round
                              Harlequin
                              The Jolly Herring
                              Someone's Singing, Lord
                              Ta-ra-ra boom-de-ay

2 **BBC books**:   *Come and Praise*

3 **Ward Lock Educational**: *Every Colour Under the Sun*

4 **Out of the Ark Music**:   *Songs for Every Day*
                              Songs for Every Season

As suggested in the introduction to the book, the following list is a
summary of the songs used in this book and is intended to save
teachers from ploughing through the assemblies to find a particular
type of song. Needless to say, all schools have their own preferred
song-books and it is a matter of choice as to which songs, if any, are
used in the assemblies in this book.

Songs suggested for 'Special Occasions' are not included in this
compilation.

Songs for general use

A better world	*Alleluya* 60
A living song	*Come & Praise* 72
A still, small voice	*Come & Praise* 96
A time for everything	*Songs for Every Day* p 25
All night, all day	*Alleluya* 75
All the nations of the earth	*Come & Praise* 14
Calypso	*Flying a Round* 68
Can you hear	*Harlequin* 33
Do your best	*Every Colour* 48

Don't you think we're lucky?	*Every Colour* 25
Each day different	*Harlequin* 43
For all the strength	*Every Colour* 17
He gave me eyes	*Someone's Singing, Lord* 19
I come like a beggar	*Come & Praise* 90
I may speak	*Come & Praise* 100
It's a new day	*Come & Praise* 106
Look around	*Every Colour* 9
Maja pade – let's all be happy	*Tinderbox* 57
Monday morning	*Songs for Every Day* p 6
Morning has broken	*Someone's Singing, Lord* 3
Morning sun	*Come & Praise* 93
Mysteries	*Tinderbox* 40
O Lord! Shout for joy!	*Someone's Singing, Lord* 4
On life's highway	*Every Colour* 48
One more step	*Come & Praise* 47
Seeds of kindness	*Every Colour* 42
Simple gifts	*Come & Praise* 97
Song of life	*Every Colour* 22
Somebody greater	*Come & Praise* 5
Spirit of peace	*Come & Praise* 85
Stand up, clap hands	*Someone's Singing, Lord* 14
Stick on a smile	*Every Colour* 43
Take the time to cogitate	*Every Colour* 47
Taking my time	*Songs for Every Day* p 61
The bell of creation	*Come & Praise* 86
The journey of life	*Come & Praise* 45
There's so much pleasure	*Every Colour* 10
Think, think on these things	*Someone's Singing, Lord* 38
Time is a thing	*Come & Praise* 104
To everything turn	*Come & Praise* 113
Travel on	*Come & Praise* 42
Turn, turn, turn	*Alleluya* 32
Use your eyes	*Every Colour* 11
We are climbing	*Come & Praise* 49
Work calypso	*Tinderbox* 23
You shall go out with joy	*Come & Praise* 48
You've got to move	*Come & Praise* 107
Water of life	*Come & Praise* 2
When a knight won his spurs	*Come & Praise* 50

A small ark

God created them all	*Songs for Every Day* p 54
Rabbit ain't got	*Apusskidu* 37
Song of the frogs	*Flying a Round* 21
When a dinosaur's feeling hungry	*Tinderbox* 12

Friends and neighbours

Both sides now	*Alleluya* 33
Because you care	*Every Colour* 31
Every colour under the sun	*Every Colour* 16
I was lying in the road	*Come & Praise* 88
If I had a hammer	*Every Colour* 40
Love somebody	*Tinderbox* 16
Side by side	*Ta-ra-ra-boom-de-ay* 36
Such hard work	*Every Colour* 29
Sing a song of people	*Tinderbox* 18
Take care of a friend	*Every Colour* 35
Thank you for my friends	*Tinderbox* 31
The hungry man	*Every Colour* 32
We will take care of you	*Every Colour* 36
When I needed a neighbour	*Come & Praise* 65
Working together	*Every Colour* 37
Would you turn your back?	*Every Colour* 34
You and I	*Tinderbox* 56

House and home

Grandfather's clock	*Ta-ra-ra-boom-de-ay* 54
Hands to work	*Someone's Singing, Lord* 21
'Losing things' song	*Songs for Every Day* p 42
Place to be	*Tinderbox* 34
The building song	*Alleluya* 59

I am a person

Don't you push me down	*Tinderbox* 26
I can climb	*Come & Praise* 50
I may speak	*Come & Praise* 100
I whistle a happy tune	*Apusskidu* 3
On a work day I work	*Every Colour* 24

One, two, three	*Tinderbox* 65
My mind to me a kingdom is	*Every Colour* 18

The world around us

All things bright and beautiful	*Come & Praise* 3
Bread for the world	*Come & Praise* 73
Give to us eyes	*Someone's Singing, Lord* 18
In the bustle of the city	*Come & Praise* 101
Let the world rejoice together	*Come & Praise* 14
Milk bottle tops and paper bags	*Someone's Singing, Lord* 17
Pollution	*Jolly Herring* 19
Pollution calypso	*Every Colour* 16
Roller skating	*Harlequin* 23
The world is big	*Tinderbox* 33
Wheels keep turning	*Apusskidu* 24

What a life!

All the world's a roundabout	*Alleluya* 33
Give to us eyes	*Every Colour* 11
Hayho! Time to go to bed!	*Flying a Round* 14
It's a great, great shame	*Every Colour* 44
Points of view	*Every Colour* 45
Taking my time	*Songs for Every Day* p 61
This way that a-way	*Come & Praise* 53
Travel on	*Come & Praise* 42
Try again	*Tinderbox* 56

Appendix IV:

Are you listening, God?

Prayers for all occasions

Dear God, we shall have this day only once. Help us not to waste one minute of it.

Lord, teach us to respect other people and to care about their happiness.

Father God, please teach us how to tell right from wrong and how to stand up for all that is good.

Lord God, make us brave when we are afraid and to call on you when we are in trouble.

Lord of the universe, thank you for our world. Show us how to care for our environment and for all living things that depend upon it.

Father of us all, help us to do all the good we can in all the ways we can.

Thank you, God, for our health and strength. Show us the best way to help those who are neither healthy nor strong.

Dear Father of us all, remind us from time to time that we cannot do what we like whenever we like and wherever we like, but that we should always consider the well-being of others.

It's only me, Lord

Dear Lord, give me courage when I am afraid.

Father, please forgive me when I have done wrong and help me to forgive others when they have offended me.

Dear Lord, please forgive me for the times when I have turned my backs on others when they have needed my help.

Father God, remind me now and again that it is wiser to tell the truth than to tell lies.

Lord, as we begin another day,
Guide me in all I do and say.
Let me harm no person here,
But end the day with conscience clear.

The people around us

Lord of us all, help all those people who are sad or worried today. Father, please give your strength to those who are alone and afraid.

Father, be good to those people who do not have enough to eat.

Father, comfort those people who are ill, whether at home or in hospital.

Father God, bless children everywhere and keep them safe from harm.

Thank you, Lord, for the people who care for us when we are ill.

Lord, please support and care for those men and women who protect us when danger is about.

Father, we thank you for all those men and women who work to provide us with all our daily needs.

Father, we thank you for all those who keep our environment safe and clean.

The world about us

Thank you, Father, for flowers and trees and all things that grow in our parks and gardens.

Father, teach us to care for and to respect our surroundings.

Lord, teach us never to take risks on the roads or in the places where we play.

Father, teach us to be kind to animals, whether they are pets or wild creatures.

Lord, help us to care for our villages, towns and cities so that they may be better places in which to live.

This is our school

Thank you, God, for our school and for all those who help us here.

Help us, Lord, to make our school a happy and safe place for all who come here.

We thank you, Father God, for our teachers and all who help us to learn.

Thank you, Father, for those who keep our school clean and comfortable and for those who prepare, serve and supervise our meals. Teach us, Father, to be proud of our school and show us what we can do to make it even better.

A school creed

This is our school,
Let peace live here,
Let the rooms be full of happiness,
Let love be all around,
Love of one another,
Love of all people
And love of life and living.
Let us remember
That as many hands build a house,
So many hearts build a school.
This school creed is set to music on page 210.

A child's prayer (based on The Lord's Prayer)

Father, who is everywhere,
Your name is special to us.
Be with us now and always.
With your help
May we always do what is right.
Help us to feed the world.
We regret doing wrong things,
For which we ask you to forgive us
And we will try to forgive those who have hurt us.
Protect us from wickedness and wicked people
And teach us how to make the best of life.

The Lord's Prayer (contemporary language version based on Matthew 6, New English Bible, 1970)

Our Father in heaven,

your name is holy,

your kingdom come,

your will be done

on earth as in heaven.

Give us today our daily bread.

Forgive us the wrong we have done,

As we have forgiven those who have wronged us.

And do not bring us to the test,

But save us from evil,

For yours is the kingdom

and the power and the glory, for ever.

Amen

Blessings for the close of assembly

Lord, be with us through today. Help us to do what is right.

Father, help us to do our best today and to be as helpful as we can.

Bless us, Father God, and care for us all through this coming day.

Dear God, help us to be sensible and responsible children through the day that is before us.

Prayers for the close of school

O let us see another day;
Bless us this night we pray
And to the sun we all will bow
And say 'Goodbye', but just for now.

(from Eli Jenkins' prayer, 'Under Milk Wood', by Dylan Thomas)

Lord, keep us safe this night,
Strengthened by your power,
No fears to keep us from our rest
Through all the night's dark hours.

Father, you are with us as we sleep,

Secure from all our fears,
For you are with us through the night
'Til morning light appears.

Now the day is over,
Night is drawing near,
Lord, guard us as we rest tonight,
And take away all fear.

Blessings for the close of school

Father, care for us as we make our way home.
We thank you, Lord, for this day at school. Be with us as we go home.
Lord, thank you for our day at school and for all that we have learnt.
Bless us all, our Father, and be with us as we go home.

Appendix V

Useful assembly books for Years 3 to 6

Active Assemblies for the National Curriculum	Iracey & Dinsdale	Schofield & Sims
Assemblies A-Z	Ward	Stanley Thornes
Assemblies for Primary Schools (Autumn, Spring and Summer terms, 3 books)	Cooling	Religious & Moral Press(RMEP)
It's Our Assembly (It's our turn for assembly)	Rarncombe	National council for Christian education (NCEC)
The Autumn Assembly Book	Brandling	Stanley Thornes
The Spring Assembly Book	Brandling	Stanley Thornes
The Winter Assembly Book	Brandling	Stanley Thornes
Assembly Kit	Wood	Longman
Day by Day	Purton	Basil Blackwell
Good morning, Everybody! (Years 3 and 4)	Brandling	Stanley Thornes
Many Hearts (Year 3)	Davies	Nash Pollock
Share our World	Jackson	Stanley Thornes
Through the Year	Wilcock	Stanley Thornes
Tinderbox Assembly Book	Barrett	A & C Black
Together Today	Fisher	Evans
A World of Light	Price & Parmiter	Schofield & Sims

Wisdom for Worship (based on the Book of Proverbs)	Cooling	Stapleford Project

Further suggestions for song books

Children Praising	OUP
Come and Sing	Scripture Union
Hymns and Songs for Children	National Society
Mango Spice (Caribbean songs)	A & C Black
Morning has Broken	Schofield & Sims
Sing a Song 1 and 2	Nelson
Songs of Praise	OUP
Ta-ra-ra-boom-de-ay	A & C Black
Sing a Song of Celebration	Holt, Rinehard & Winston

Festivals and celebrations

Musical calendar of festivals	Ward Lock
Sing a Song of Celebrations	General Holt, Rinehard & Winston
Merrily to Bethlehem	A & C Black
Oxford Book of Carols	OUP